Mules, Jackasses
and Other
Misconceptions

James Austin Burkhart
and
Eugene Francis Schmidtlein

Stephens College
Columbia, Mo.

D1213771

Preface

When Professor James A. Burkhart came to Missouri and Stephens College in 1944, he looked for a local subject that would fascinate him and provide a good research area. The mule became that subject and for the next thirty five years Jim Burkhart searched high and low for information and interpretations of the mule's role in American life and development. He particularly enjoyed talking with the people who raised, worked or traded mules. He loved to listen to their language and vivid descriptions.

Upon retirement, he was going to write his Mule Book. Many ideas, facts, and stories were already recorded. But his life ended abruptly with cancer.

When I retired in 1992, I asked Mrs. June Burkhart if she would let me go through Jim's research so that the book could be finished. What fun I have had reading all of the material Jim had collected over 35 years.

My debts in this project are many. I particularly thank June, Deirdre and Jim for letting me do this. Melvin Bradley has been completely unselfish in sharing his knowledge and experience with mules. His eight volumes of interviews are a wonderful resource for mule lovers.

Burkhart gave many talks and wrote a number of newspaper and magazine articles on mules. From his notes and typed copy, it was sometimes impossible for me to determine what was his composition and what was taken from other authors. I have tried to acknowledge every source I could and I apologize if there are sources used of which I am unaware.

My family and friends have endured my preoccupation with mules in a very patient manner. My wife, Mary, has been extremely helpful and long suffering throughout this project. Uncle Jack has provided advice and encouragement. Mule fever overcame him as it did me. Rachel suffered through teaching me the intracacies of the computer for which I cannot thank her adequately.

Introduction

Unlike Americans who are witnessing their first millennium, it is possible that the mule will be observing its eighth millennium. It is significant that the mule has endured through all these millennia and that it continues to kick up its heels as the next one begins. The mule is one of the few animals that can die, become extinct, and then be reborn. This phoenix capability has caused a sense of mystery about the mule, something special and unique in the works of creation. Some Missourians even question the fact of mules dying. They claim the mule is immortal and indestructible. One Ozarkian said he remembered seeing a mule that was clearly branded: "B.C."

Missouri is the geographical and cultural heart of everyday America and the common people. The genius of Mark Twain captured this reality and thus he was honored as "the Mirror of America." The mule is such a mirror too.

Missouri has been called the "Show Me State." Missourians tend to be skeptical and questioning. Sometimes this tendency can be misconstrued as stubbornness, but it is really something different. It means a carefulness and a demand for evidence to prove that something is true or that a situation is safe to enter.

Like the mule, Missourians are often the butt of New York and California jokes for being slow and behind the times. These outsiders would even say that "living in Missouri" was a contradiction. This ridicule is endured with a certain amount of patience and humility, recognizing that hard work and perseverance will win acclaim eventually. In a parallel manner, the equine caste system clearly made the mule inferior to the horse and relegated the mule to heavy labor and the tasks of the subservient class.

This scorn and adversity forged the "greatness" of the mule. William Faulkner hardly could have made his praise of the mule more effusive than his statement in Sartoris:

"Some Homer of the cotton fields should sing the saga of the mule and of his place in the South. He it was, more than any other creature or thing, who, steadfast to the land when all else faltered before the hopeless juggernaut of circumstance, impervious to conditions that broke men's hearts because of his venomous and patient preoccupation with the immediate present, won the prone South from beneath the iron heel of Reconstruction and taught it pride again through humility, and courage through adversity overcome; who accomplished the well nigh impossible despite hopeless odds, by sheer and vindictive patience."

Another southerner, Ralph McGill, once the renowned editor of the *Atlanta Constitution,* wrote: "The mule is so much like man—ornery, stubborn, friendly, willing, a worker—that people love him. Folks sort of feel a kinship with a mule. So I hope as progress keeps progressing, some place will be found for the mule."

For many reasons then, Americans need to know what a mule is, how to recognize it when one sees it, and be familar with the process of manufacturing one. The mule is and has been joined intimately with American politics and jurisprudence. Likewise, it has many connections with American businesses, large and small. The mule also has a long military record and has served with great distinction.

In fact, the mule's history is rich and multifaceted. It is so rich and illustrious that it lends itself well to legendmaking and storytelling which is a characteristic of greatness in history.

Not only do Americans and Missourians know that the mule is something distinctive and will survive beyond the next millennium, people in other countries know it too. A Swiss newspaper, not long ago, carried an article with the following headline: "Das Muli ist noch langst nicht ausgestorben." (The mule is not yet extinct.) The article was accompanied by a photo of a Swiss farmer leading his loaded mule through a narrow street.

Maybe the greatest contribution of the mule has been in the important area of humor. Just the mention of mules or jackasses will cause people to smile. Jokes and stories are plentiful. Everyone who has worked with them has a special feeling that he or she wants to talk about and share.

The next millennium will see the mule survive and the future generations will find new uses for the remarkable animal. The mule's hardiness and adaptability will be advantageous for the many unforeseen frontiers and new opportunities.

Table Of Contents

Chapter   Page

—— **Chapter One** ——

"What Is A Mule?"

"What is a mule? A Mule is a mule and that's all of it."

Fifty years ago, Bing Crosby answered the question in a song from the movie, "Going My Way": "A Mule is an animal with long funny ears, he kicks up at everything he hears, his back is brawny and his brain is weak, he's just plain stupid with a stubborn streak, and, if you hate to go to school, you may grow up to be a mule." So it has been throughout history for the mule. If the song had added something about meanness and something about his questionable ancestry, the caricature would be more or less complete. The poor mule has been vilified and maligned so much through the centuries that it is difficult for some observers to take it seriously.

No small part of this misunderstanding is due to the fact that God had nothing to do with the manufacture of the mule; it is completely man's doing. Some have said that it was the first bionic creature. No wonder that the mule is so hard to define, explain and understand.

This confusion over the mule has a long history reaching back into ancient times, The Greeks struggled with the mule's nature since they called him by several names: hemione or half-ass; oreos or mountain animal to haul wood; and muchlos or breeding ass. Perhaps the confusion over the meaning and derivation of the name reflects certain mysteries and ambiguities in the animal's biological make-up.

In loose, unscientific terms, the mule is spawned by a male ass, or jackass, and the reluctant female horse or mare. The word mare presumably comes from the Anglo-Saxon myre or mere, a word which originally meant increase, and "more," and later was used to indicate the female sex of any powerful animal. The result of this potent mixture, the mule, has a libido and gender all its own.

Interestingly, the mule can be of either sex, male or female, but, unlike the horse and the ass, the union of the male and female mule is

1

without issue. Both the male mule, often called the horse mule, and the female mule, often called the mare mule, have the proper equipment, education, information and inclination for sexual reproduction. In fact, they engage in sexual relations without incurring any future obligations or responsibilities. With these characteristics, the mule would be perfect for the present day's unlimited attention to sex for pleasure or irresponsible sex. With only a handful of authenticated exceptions, the mule is sterile.

Likewise, the inverted breeding equation, the male horse and the female ass, is without issue. The cross between a stallion and the jennet or jenny (female ass) contributes another hybrid to the animal kingdom, the hinny. This name comes from hinnire, to hinny, whinny or neigh. Animals were often named after the sound they made or from some peculiar characteristic. The hinny neighs like a horse, while the mule brays like an ass. The hinny has been relatively rare on the American landscape while the mule has been created many times over.

The baffling infertility of the mule has provided rich material for many comedians and jokesters, including political pundits. Ignatius Donnelly, a well known political figure after the Civil War, drew the mule and its Papa into American politics so permanently that the connection is still very evident today on editorial pages of our news media. Donnelly derisively proclaimed: "The Democratic Party is like a mule, without pride of ancestry or hope of posterity." Now why would the mule be so cursed as to be associated with a political party?

This association of the donkey and mule with the Democratic Party must have been effective with the American people because Thomas Nast, the famous cartoonist, picked it up quickly and he contributed greatly to the donkey becoming the symbol of the Democrats.

Theodore H. Savory, a scientific writer, tried to defend the jackass by saying that Donnelly was unfair and inaccurate in the statement. The Populist leader was unfair because most breeders take great care in selecting both parents so there can be pride of ancestry. He was inaccurate because female mules have been known to produce foals. It is rare but it can happen.

Because of the ridicule, unfairness and injustice, the mule and donkey (the mule's father) have had to endure much abuse, even much physical abuse. Charles Dickens alluded to this fact and had difficulty understanding how people could be so cruel and think nothing wrong in such behavior.

Once Dickens attended a market wherein every imaginable animal and object was being put up for sale, including a hundred or so donkeys. Dickens wrote that the costermonger gave vent to all his varied feelings by whacking on the donkey standing beside him. If he was angry, happy, or in between, he would whack the donkey. He even invited others to whack away if it so suited them. Dickens couldn't believe the cruelty especially since the donkeys were well behaved.

Sometimes one wonders if the difficulty of defining the mule is simply because people believe that such a question does not deserve serious attention. Ray Lum was a renowned mule and horse trader and, deep down, had an affection for the mule. But when asked, "What is a mule?" Lum replied with a curt statement: "Oh, it's one of those hard tails."

Mules were called hard tails because their tails were shaved. This practice drew the mule into the further infamy of being associated with an Army Second Lieutenant who is called, among other names, a "shave tail." The men serving under him often thought he was a jackass.

The peculiar nature of the mule has provoked endless thought and conjecture even among Missourians. Down in the Ozarks, so the story goes, a group of intelligentsia mulled over the riddle of the mule to view it from as many vantage points as possible. Each homegrown philosopher tried to outsmart the others in thought as well as in language. The first old timer swallowed his tobacco and cleared his drawling voice, "A mule is a mule and when you've gone and sed that, you've done sed all thar's to say, except to say, he's a stout animal."

The second pundit rose from his nail keg chair: "God is s'pposed to have made all things, but he done forgot about the mule. Even them that's make the mule won't admit it. The mule's own maw is ashamed of him and his paw disowns him. The mule's papa, the Jackass, and the mama, the mare, wiln't live together. He's made in rape and out of wedlock. The mule is a pure and simple bastard. He excels in sleuth and cunning. He'll love yuh ta death for twenty years just to kick yuh. The only thing his lame brains understand is curses and the cudgel. He is at his best behavior when he's being down right whupped. The mule will live longer on less than any other animal. And thar's a reason for it. A mule is just too down right mean to die. The mule is so dang stubborn, he weren't cooperate with man ner nature to help make hisself over again."

Another country-wit took the floor and spoke very deliberately:

3

"A mule is nature's puzzlement. He is like a big, near-ready persimmon. Looks sound on the outside but watch out for all hell's gonna break loose. The mule is always sideways with himself and always otherwise with other people. He is wise and foolish, lofty and lowly, grand and grouchy. n short, the mule is a sugar 'n spice mix of virtue and vice. He's nature's dynamite. He ain't even good enough to get in the zoo. Noah wouldn't let him in the Ark cause he ain't got no mate and cause the devil hisself was with 'em. He weren't present at the dawn of creation and he'll be AWOL as twilight descends on Judgment Day. This celebrated reprobate will forever be praised and damned, whupped and fergiven and whupped again."

The most learned and articulate resident, a former school-teacher, followed: "The mule is an outrage upon nature, a combination of the donkey and the horse, with the qualities of neither and excelling both. He is the puzzle of the brutes, and stands alone in his nature and qualities, unapproachable in devilment, fathomless in cunning, born old in crime, of disreputable paternity and incapable of posterity, stolid, imperturbable, with no love for anything but the perpetration of tricks, no dexterity in aught save the flinging of his heels, no desire for anything but rations—stolen if possible and by preference—and no affection at all. Such is the mule."

The fifth speaker was a real cracker-barrel thinker who had been doin' more listenin' than talkin'. He began: "Holy Toledo! I dunno what all them thar high falutin words meant but I say, I take my facts from my King James and my Ozark Dictionary. When temptation strikes, my King James tells me to take the lesser of the evils. When my mule strikes, my Ozark Dictionary tells me, 'git! and don't sure-as-hell turn the other cheek.' Where he kicks, I make sure that's where I was. I suspicioned a windy conversation like this might come up. So like Mister Teacher thar, I done my homework. I looked up the definition of a mule in my Ozark Dictionary. I thumbed to the word 'mule' and it sez, 'See Burro'. I paged to 'burro' and it sez, an Arizona Nightingale or Desert Canary, frequently referred to as Knobhead or Jughead and other words that are unprintable here, Spanish for Donkey, see Donkey. I went to the word 'Donkey' and larnt, 'An object commonly found on the front picture of postcards, the father of a mule', an 'ass', see 'Jackass'. I looked up the word 'jackass' and it sez, 'a stupid person', 'specially a person who dern't know what a 'jackass' is, the father of a mule, 'see onager'. I found this, 'often used in Crossword Puzzles, a wild ass (which is about as redundant as one can be), see hybrid. I turned to the word Hybrid and discovered what it all meant and what a mule actually war. The dictionary sez, 'Hybrid,' a synonym for 'mule' 'mule,' a cross between a "Jackass,' among other things, and a mare who ain't none too particular'."

This sparkling conversation stirred the author's curiosity further so he consulted his new edition of the Random House Dictionary. Under mule, it said: any sterile hybrid; a small locomotive used for pulling rail cars as in a coal yard or on an industrial site, or for towing, as of ships through canal locks. Spinning mule: a machine for spinning cotton or other fibres into yarn and winding the yarn on spindles. Mule Canary: a hybrid between a canary and a finch. Mule: a lounging slipper that covers the toes and instep or only the instep. Mule Deer: a large western North American deer with large ears and a brown coat.

There are mules and then there are more mules. There are cotton mules, tobacco mules, logging mules, mining mules, pack mules, wagon mules, levee mules, farm mules, sugar mules, jumping mules, racing mules, show mules, strawberry mules, miniature mules, riding mules, draft mules, horse mules, mare mules, molly mules, gelding mules, stallion mules, coon hunting mules, and on and on.

Missouri produced and marketed all kinds and sizes of mules just like Detroit later produced and marketed all kinds and sizes of cars and trucks, so wrote Peter Chew in the *Smithsonian*,

To some observers, the mule is the son of Beelzebub. He is a malediction. He is a most-slandered animal. Some think he is ornery, hammer-heeled, bafflebrained, in addition to being misbegotten.

Yet the mule has charisma. He attracts attention. Some say he has 'color'. He can certainly make one see black and blue and red. William Faulkner said he was hell-born and hell-returnin'. People smile upon the mention of his name. Many farmers who owned and worked horses and mules seem to recall the mules more vividly and fondly. They are also more likely to recall their names. The mule's impression was more indelible for many reasons.

A moving tribute to the mule's father, the donkey, was contained in a fable from a vision of St. Francis of Assisi. Louis Untermeyer related it very beautifully. The story had to do with Jesus's entry into Jerusalem before his death. Such a triumphal entry had to be celebrated in an appropriate manner. The archangel called all the animals before Jesus so he make his choice. The lion argued his case as the king of beasts. The eagle answered by pointing out to what heights of

5

power and grandeur it could carry our Lord on its wings.

The elephant pointed out that it was the oldest of animals and possessed true wisdom which every ruler needed. The cow informed Jesus that it was a sacred animal in India and Egypt and that it fed the world. The horse begged selection because of its speed.

After all the animals had made their case before Jesus, there was only one animal which had remained silent. Jesus turned to the donkey and asked what it could offer. "Nothing," said the donkey, "I am just a humble creature." Consequently, Jesus chose to ride upon the ass as he entered Jerusalem.

The fable ends with Jesus marking on the back of the ass a black cross which ran down the back and from shoulder to shoulder and is still there today.

Since Jesus's entry into Jerusalem was such a special event in the ass family, other writers have honored it as well. G.K. Chesterton wrote a poem, The Donkey:

When fishes flew and forests walked
And figs grew upon thorn,
Some moment when the moon was blood
Then surely I was born.
With monstrous head and sickening cry
And ears like errant wings,
The Devil's walking parody
On all four footed things.
The tattered outlaw of the earth
Of ancient crooked will:
Starve, scourge, deride me; I am dumb,
I keep my secret still.
Fools! For I had my hour;
One far fierce hour and sweet;
There was a shout about my ears,
And palms before my feet.

When Norman Garstin was writing a book on *The Horse and Our Civilization*, he stated that current civilization was built on the horse. So closely was medieval life tied to the horse that a whole social system went by the name of chivalry. Someone asked him what would have happened if society had followed the donkey instead of the horse. "In that case," Garstin answered with a smile, "we might have had a Christian civilization."

No discussion of the mule's definition would be complete without the opinion of Josh Billings. (Like many beginning writers, Josh had trouble at the start of his career getting published. Finally, at the urging of a friend, he rewrote his stories with a very creative spelling. From then on, he never had trouble.) "The mule is haf hoss and haf jackass, and thier kums two full stop, natur discoverin' her mistake.

"Twa weigh more, a kordin tu thier heft, than enny other kreetur, except a crowbar. Tha kant hear enny quicker, not further than the hoss, yet thier ears are big enuff for snow shoes.

"You kan trust them with enny one whose life aint worth any more than the mule's. The only wa to keep mules in a pstr is tu turn hem into a mudder jinling, and then jump out. "Tha are ready to use, just as soon as tha will du to abuse.

"Tha hain't got enny friends, and will eat on huckle berry brush with an ocksional change to Kanada thistles.

"Tha are a modern invenshun. I don't think the Bible deludes to them atall.

"Tha sel for more money than any domestic animile. Yo kant tell thier age by lookin' in thier mouth enny more than you kould a Mexican cannon. Tha never hav no disease that a good club won't heil.

"If tha die tha kim rite to life agin, for I never heard anybody sa 'ded mule'.

"Tha are like some men, verry korrupt at hart, ive known 'em to be good mules for six months, just to get a good chanse to kick somebody.

"I never owned one, nor ever mean to, unless thar is a United States law passed requirin' it.

"The only reason why tha are pashint is bekause tha are ashamed of themselfs. I have seen eddikated mewels in a sirkus.

"Tha kould kick, and bite, tremanjisi, would not sa what I am forced to sa agin the mewel, if his birth warn't an outrage, and man warn't tu blame for it.

"Enny man who is willin' to drive a mule ought to be exempt by law from runnin' for the legislatur.

"Tha aare the straygest creture on earth, and heavis ackordin' tu thier size. I herd tell how one who fell op from the tow path on the Eri Kanal, and sunk as soon as he touched bottom, but he kept rite on towin' the boat tu the next stashion, breathin' thru his ears, which stuck out of the water about two feet, 6 inches. I didn't see this did, but an auctioneer told me about it and I never knew an auctioneer to lie unless it was absolutely convenient."

One should observe that Josh said that mules don't really die. It is interesting when mule people start telling stories, the concept of "resurrection" quickly creeps into their conversation.

Once an Army Post held an auction of obsolete and condemned government mules. One of the mules was so outrageously bad that the auctioneer humorously, but accurately, christened him, Lazarus. after the Bible references. The animal had so many sores that he looked like a spotted mule. On top of the sores, the creature appeared to be at death's doorstep, if not already inside.

To the vocal misgivings of the crowd, Joe Felmer bought the mule. In fact, he purchased the animal with considerable enthusiasm. Amid the jeers and cheers, someone inquired of Joe: "Aren't you afraid the Apaches will get 'em?"

Joe replied: "That's jest what I buyin' him fer: bait. 'n Apache 'll come down in my alfalfy field and git thet mewel, 'n fust thing you know thar'll be a joke on somebody." Joe had a reputation for being a sharpshooter. Everybody just naturally assumed that any misguided Indian who disregarded good sense and attempted to steal a plug mule would end up close to the ground, if not under it.

However, after taking one look at Lazarus, most people felt nothing was going to happen since the mule would not last long enough to be a decoy. But they were wrong. The flee-bitten, sore-ridden, broken-down mule refused to live down to their expectations by dying. He was "resurrected" in the alfalfa and young barley; he actually improved himself.

About a month later, Joe Felmer was aroused rudely from his siesta by his work hands shouting: "Apaches, Apaches!" Joe ran to the window. Lo and behold, there was Lazarus risen from the dead. On his back sat three braves. Paralyzed with astonishment, Joe couldn't fire a shot. Soon the mule was out of range. It needed no urging. "Lazarus" looked like a high speed racer, jumping arroyos and any other obstacle in his way.

Such stories were plentiful in rural America. Mules were so much a part of rural life that stories relating to them were woven into everyday speech and cultural folklore. Oldtimers would ask for a "mule's ear of coffee", meaning, a big cup, or, a cup of coffee with a "mule's kick in it." Others would ask for a quart of Missouri "muleshine" or "white mule."

Because almost all mules in the nineteenth century were black, most young men didn't know what a "white mule" was until they tasted it.

Despite all the humor and ridicule, another important point in understanding what a mule is has to do with the fact that the Missouri mule was quite intelligent. He was often smarter than his owner. This might explain why so many owners had trouble workin' their mules. George Washington Carver said that he never saw a mule that didn't look like he thought he was thinking. Carl Russell, a native Missourian, marvelled at some of the complex tasks his mules could perform so easily. Russell said they were as smart as he was because, after all, they had gone to the same school and teacher.

So many stories and jokes belittled the mule. This tendency probably indicated that the humans were actually no match for this gifted animal and were trying to hide their inferiority by ridiculing the mule.

A classic story of the mule outsmartin' a man has received a wide telling. A farmer was talkin' to his mule, Bill, at the end of a hard day.

"I'm a man made in the image of God and you're a mule, the son of a jackass. Yet, here we are, hitched up together year in and year out. I often wonder if I work for you or you for me. I think it is a partnership between a mule and a fool, for surely I work as hard as you do, if not harder. Plowing or cultivating, we cover the same ground, but you do it on four legs, and I on two. Therefore I walk twice as much as you do.

"Soon we'll be preparing for a corn crop. When the crop is harvested, I will give one-third to the landlord for being so kind as to let me use this small speck of God's universe.

"One-third goes to me and one-third to you, Bill. I must divide my third among seven children, six hens, two ducks, the banker, and my wife. You consume all of your third by yourself.

"If we both need shoes, you get them. You're clearly getting the better of me and I ask you, is it fair for a mule, the son of jackass, to swindle a man, the lord of creation, out of his substance?

"Why, you only help to plow and cultivate, while I must cut, shock, and husk the corn. All year long, I have to worry about paying taxes, buying new harness for you, and paying the mortgage interest. And you, what do you care about taxes and mortgage interest?

"About the only time I am your superior is on election day for I can vote and you can't. After the election, I realize that I was as big a jackass as your Papa. I am prone to wonder if politics were made for men or for jackasses or to make jackasses out of men.

"And that's not all Bill. When you are dead, that's supposed to be the end of you. But me! The preacher tells me that when I die, I may go to hell forever. That's it Bill, if I don't do just as they say. And most of what they say is what I don't do. And what they say not to do, I do. I'm in trouble and you're off scot free.

"Truly, Bill, I wonder how you can keep a straight face and look so innocent and solemn."

—— **Chapter Two** ——

"The Making of The Mule"

In utter amazement, a lady asked a farmer how he was able to "raise" such big, heavy mules. With a devilish smile, he replied: "Oh, it's easy, I use jacks."

The crossing of a horse and an ass to produce a mule was more than just another case of livestock breeding. Mule making was a strange and erotic act with many preconceptions. Was not the contrived commerce between the female horse and the male ass the original sin against nature? Did not the Bible warn against the sowing of mingled seed and the gendering of cattle with diverse kinds? Was not the mule a cosmic error?

Nature apparently thought so since she refused to permit the mule to repeat the error. In fact, there were those who swore that the mule was never meant to be because the intractable creature is one animal God never made. Man alone must take the responsibility for "forcing this issue."

The biology of a mule is mysterious. Not only is the animal's conception curiously contrived but the period of gestation is protracted. It would appear that even in the embryonic stage the mule is a stubborn animal, so stubborn he refuses to be born. The making of a mule takes slightly longer than the incubation of a horse. Under these circumstances, and others, spectators to the act of the mule's creation sensed that they were privy to an unparalleled animal passion play, a drama in which the jack played the role of the villain. The mare, of course, portrayed the innocent maiden. Sometimes a stallion was used as a teaser or a stand-in and was deprived of his lady love by circumstance and the establishment.

For centuries the ass and sexuality have been tied together and have inspired much humor and cleverness. A nineteenth century limerick provides a good example:

> There was a young woman named Glass
> Who had a most beautiful ass,
> Not round and pink
> As you might think,
> But gray, and had ears, and ate grass.

The Romans were well aware of the versatile genius of the jackass and acknowledged both his sexual talent as well as his "assinine" character. For devilment, friends placed the insignia of the ass over a newly married couple's wedding bed.

In a more extraordinary relationship, the ass was linked with Typhon, the counterpart of the Egyptian ass god, Seth. Typhon had the magical faculty to cause evil to others. Many Greek and Roman chariot racers implored the Typhon to use his diabolical powers upon their rivals. These charioteers had Typhon's image engraved on lead plaques which they threw at their competitors during the race hoping to cause an accident.

During the Middle Ages, the cuckolded man, with his unfaithful wife standing by, was paraded through the streets riding backward on an ass. In certain Germanic states, the ass was associated with the doubting apostle Thomas, the saint who achieved immortality by being the last apostle to believe in the resurrection of Jesus. This association continued into this century; in Westphalia, Mo., the last boy to arrive at school on the feast of St. Thomas was greeted derisively as "Ass Thomas".

Getting back to the making of a mule, in any alliance between two animals, especially two animals of different species, farmers assumed that the male was the main contributor to the mating. As a consequence, in mule breeding, the jack was selected with utmost care. Mule raisers wanted jacks who had blood, style, size and ruggedness.

In Roman times, Columella wrote: "Many stallions which are admirable as far as appearance goes procreate offspring which are very inferior…, while some stallions which have been despised on account of their appearance are productive of the most valuable progeny." Still as the jack stock industry grew and blooded jacks were registered in the American Jack and Jennet Registry, an ideal prototype developed as the kind of jack likely to win blue ribbons in the show ring and to produce good mule colts on the farm.

A prime jack should run as tall as 15 to 16 hands and weigh 1,000 to 1,200 pounds. In addition, the model animal should have a straight and strong back, smooth but heavily muscled hips, a well developed rump; he should be heavy boned, have well-shaped shoulders, a thick, broad chest, deep-set ribs, and a rather large head. A critical factor which never seemed to change was the length of the jack's ears. Breeders measured the ears not with a twelve inch ruler but with a yardstick. Good ears were long and erect, but not too thick. When spread sideways, ears which reached 36 inches or a whole yardstick from tip to tip were not uncommon.

Throughout the peak of the mule age, farmers dealt mainly in black jacks and when they got one with a white nose, it was a winner. Grey jacks seemed to father grey mules. These animals eventually turned even more hoary with age, and, as a result, farmers and army remount recruiters shunned the ghostly specters. Moreover, in many farming and mining communities, the white mule and the white jack were regarded as ghosts connected to evil happenings. (In rural Mississippi, it was just the opposite; a white mule meant good luck.)

Many miners refused to work in the same mine with a white mule. Who could blame them? Imagine turning a sharp curve in a black tunnel and seeing a grotesque figure with long, white ears looming in the darkness.

Today jacks are ass-essed solely upon the basis of color and the favored color is red or sorrel. In the show ring, a sorrel mule with a white mane is the right color. As one mule show judge put it, "I like all women and some mules, but in both women and mules, I like redheads best." Actually, sorrels, besides being pretty, are uniform in color, which facilitates matching them in teams. Gene Chipman of Perry, Mo., a famed mule raiser and trainer, explained the secret of success in mule competition: "What you want in a mule today is a lady that stands about 15.1 hands or 61 inches, with a short back, and that nice firmness—and as blond as blond can be."

Unfortunately for the mule, the care in the selection of his maternal bloodline was never as rigorous as the textbooks in animal husbandry recommended. Experts bewailed the common practice of using second class mares as brood mares. It was unbelievable that stock raisers would breed only their best mares to a stallion worth $2,000 to $3,000, while a jack with the same price tag would be crossed with common dams.

Strong horse partisans never fully approved of mule breeding. These horse patrons would never admit that good mares crossed with good jack stock would produce a better work animal than the same mares bred to a quality stallion.

The remarkable fact about this unbalanced union (a good jack and a mediocre mare) was that the mules produced were strong and sturdy. An old and decrepit mare somehow seemed to breed better beneath herself. Mule colts from a flea-bitten, sway-backed old mare often turned out better than her natural children. The phenomenon even struck geneticists as something just short of the miraculous. Professor A.L. Hagedorn observed that it was almost incredible to see the great variety of mares and the astonishing uniformity of mule colts. Mares, differing as much as horses could possibly differ, and "the mules look as if they had been turned out by machinery."

THE COURTSHIP

Of all the games animals play, surely courtship is the most playful. In the love match leading to conception of the mule, the mare behaved like a Victorian coquette. When a mare was not in heat, she was downright frigid. Cold-blooded mares could and did resist the most subtle and persistent advances. Such a mare might show her hoofs and teeth with such ferocity that even the most aggressive jack took cover in self protection. Jacks who failed to heed the danger signals have been killed by a mare's lethal kick.

At other times, mares were apathetic, and, on still other occasions, a mare might exhibit only mild academic interest in the prospect of an affair. Nevertheless, when a mare was "ready," her lust, according to Columella, was greater than all other animals. The Roman author said "mares are affected by such a burning desire of intercourse...by imagining in their own minds the pleasure of love they become pregnant with the wind." Indeed, the poet Virgil wrote:

> But, beyond all furies, wonderous is
> the rage of mares;...facing the west,
> and the light breezes, and oft
> with wind conceive, without the aid
> of union—a wondrous tale to tell.

Since the beginning of oestrus in the mare was slower and more inconspicuous than in most, if not all of the domestic animals, only the mare knew when she was ready. The trick was to determine when the mare showed signs of "showing."

At the onset of oestrus, the mare might welcome her sexual partner. However, a brief foreplay was necessary to hasten desire. To arrive at biological consensus between the two species, the stallion was drafted for the preliminary work while the jack waited anxiously and covetously in the wings until the mare was ready.

Another exotic tint was added by calling such a stallion "proud." He was used to test, tease and titillate the mare. Such a creature was called "proud" because he had nothing to be proud of. Nature had emasculated him and he was a perfect foil in the encounter between the jack and the mare.

The stallion, proud or otherwise, was used as agent provocateur, to prepare the mare. His advances were deceptive. At a glance, the engagement between the stallion "teaser" and the mare resembled marital discord.

With neck extended and upper lip upcurled, the stallion would release a bloodcurdling mating call. He would then sniff up to the mare and nip her ears and then her withers.

Whinnying softly, the stalwart aggressor would work back to the mare's flanks. During the initial acts of this sexual ceremony, the mare often remained seemingly unmoved and quiescent.

The teasing of a mare with a stallion in preparation for union with the jack was the butt of many stories. Will Stanton, who later became a county superintendent of schools in his home county, recalled how, as a boy of 10 or 12, his father asked him to take an aged and ill-natured mare to the jack breeding station. The elder Stanton hoped that the slightly antiquated and rather pesky animal might partially redeem herself by producing one last mule colt.

Will followed his father's wishes to the "t". First he half-dragged, half-walked the vexatious mare to a nearby jack farm where the owner advertised:

JACK WHO'LL STAND AND SERVE

COVER FEE $5

MONEY BACK GUARANTEE

Arriving at the jack stand, Will repeated his father's instructions: "We want our mare bred to a jack in order to get a mule." Will paid the cover charges and got ready for the action. The man took Will's money. However, much to Will's surprise, the jack man went to the shed and came out, not with a jack, but with a stallion. The breeder then proceeded to lead the stallion toward the mare. The usually uncontrollable female was all eyes and expectation.

Will had never seen a jack cover a mare because young children were excluded from such an audience. However, many rural adolescent voyeurs would perch precariously on the branches of nearby trees and peak surreptitiously through the leaves to watch "the goings on." Will suffered from an overprotected childhood and had not seen what other boys had seen. Seeing the huge stallion and not knowing the animal was a "teaser" rather than a "breeder," Will cried out:

"Whoa. No. No. No. Not the horse. The Jackass, the Jackass, please. My Pa wants a mule colt, not a horse colt!

Pa ain't goin' to like it! I want my money back!"

A good jack received special attention and care especially as his reliability was established for producing outstanding mules. Breeders debated endlessly over his care. What feed was best? Should he be given corn?

A good jack was used just for breeding and thus he avoided all the different kinds of work imposed on mules. As one might suspect in such a situation, a jack could become "spoiled" and develop a testy disposition. If some people were afraid of mules, how much more did they tremble in the presence of a jack. One breeder complained that he could never take a vacation because he couldn't find anyone brave enough to take care of his jacks while he was gone. It took someone special to handle jacks.

Such a person was Leo F. Baumli, in northwest Missouri. For many years, he has been one of the leading jack producers in the country. His annual sales attract buyers from Canada, Mexico and all the fifty states.

First of all, Baumli looked for a big jack, close to 15 hands or 60 inches tall. "He's got to have a good back and especially good head and ears and a good hip and good straight hind legs. And don't want no jacks that will pin them ears forward at you. They gotta hold them ears up.

"Keep the young jack away from all other jennies, for sure, and grow him up with some young colts. some filly colts, either one.

Horse colts just as good. And then when he's two years old, take and use him a few times on a mare, but don't let him 'round no mules or no jennies, and I don't have no trouble breakin' a jack to breed a mare.

"Don't try to use a young jack when it's pourin' rain or a windy day. It makes a difference. That windy day is a big difference on a young jack. They'll work ten times quicker if the wind isn't blowin'. They're smart. The wind'll bother a young jack.

"I learn a jack to get ready just talkin' to him and close to the mare and I've…generally bred any jack in a few minutes and not stand around waitin' on him."

The "talkin'" was important. "I always talk to a jack and get the jack close to the mare. I'll have my left hand in his halter and my right hand to his shoulder, and I'll make him think he's gonna get to the mare and keep tellin' him to come on, come on, and then, if I have to, I got leverage with my right hand into his shoulder to pull his head, keep him from gettin' on. And the first thing, he'll be startin' to raise his tail and gettin' ready. And then I'll have the tail rope on the mare and all he's gotta do is jump. I have really good luck breakin' jacks, but I have broke a lot of jacks."

Be sure you "…don't let that jack on that mare until he is ready and make sure that you cover that mare that first time. The way my pit set up, I guarantee you when he jumps up, he'll enter the mare."

A good pit was extremely necessary for this conjunction. Baumli described his pit: "I have a good stout pit where the mare can't have any chance of gettin' out of it and the mare's standin' uphill in the pit and dropped down with her hind feet, eight inches lower than where the jack stands, and that makes it easy for that jack to get onto the mare 'cause the jack is ordinarily smaller that a big Belgian mare and that gives the advantage of him gettin' on easy which encourages him to go right ahead and get ready and breed the mare, where he don't have no trouble jumpin' right on. And where the mare's standin' uphill, it's just nature's way of enterin' the mare.

"…I have a pipe with…I got an adjustment on the right side of my jack pit that's got 5 or 6 adjustments….You stick a gas pipe in and I gotta a chain over on the side where I work from, the left side, and gotta V-iron and I got…I push that pipe back against her chest any length I want, just the thickness of the mare, back against the back of the jack pit and where she's standin' uphill and her hind feet down below, makes her rear end hang back out over the jack pit and that way, when the jack comes off of the mare, his feet never gets into the jack pit. And I tie the mare forward too, so she can't rear up or pull back and tie 'em crossways really secure. She about has to stay there. And the pit's stout enough to hold 'em too.

"The pit is made out of what we call hedge here. It's osage orange. It's somethin' that can't be broke, hardly. It's about 3 inches thick or more. I think I have an ideal jack pit. That's what I was gonna say. I copied it off of J.C. Penney's back in 1946 and every jack pit I was around. I wrote down measurements and I think I've got all the advantages in this one. I wouldn't change it anywhere right now and I've used it a lotta times this summer."

Because the tension and excitement is at such a high level all around, Baumli added strong advice to avoid kicking and biting. He often used a muzzle on the jack so that he couldn't bite the mare's neck or an attendant's arm. He could be quite vicious if one were not extra careful. "There has been some people hurt by jacks by carelessness. It was poor management that got 'em hurt."

How did Baumli feed his young jacks? "Just let 'em run the oats, full-feed oats....Just keep it in front of 'em. I don't have to feed 'em every mornin' and night then. And they don't eat much more on full-feed than they do if you just hand fed 'em.

"Try to keep grain pasture and then in the winter, good hay. No musty hay...it's not good for their lungs. I feed alfalfa...with a lot of brome or orchard grass in it. Brome and orchard grass's got a lot of protein too, and it binds their bowels up more. Makes their manure better....Don't feed corn. That corn'll heat their blood up and make 'em break out into a sore. And a jack sore, if it develops into a regular jack sore, it is kinda hard to heal, but I've got a formula that I can use that'll heal it if anything will.

"I've give it to other people, but it should be a druggist to mix it up for you. It can explode. It's 3/4 of an ounce of sulphuric acid and 1 pint of lectified (?) turpentine and 1 pint of fish oil. And you put it on once a day on a sore and it won't blister and that jack won't chew on himself where the sore is and a fly can't land near it. But it should be a druggist to mix that up or you mix that sulphuric acid by drops or it'll explode. And keep it in a glass jug. It'll get hot. When they mix it, it'll boil, but that is good medicine.

"Fifty percent Ortho for rose bushes. And that is wonderful powder to clean a sore. It'll eat it off and clean it off and make a sore heal pretty good. But it don't keep the flies away like this other medicine.

You can't smell this other. It'll take your breath. It'll shut you off right now."

As one can imagine, not all mule breeders were as systematic and careful as Leo Baumli. Sometimes a mule owner got in over his head and ended up in a heap of trouble. A well known mule trader in Tipton, Missouri, by the name of Bill McVean told about how he almost lost his life.

One summer there was a widely quoted newspaper story about a local jack that was extremely vicious. So vicious in fact that its jaw-bone reminded the citizens of Samson's biblical weapon. In a fit of frenzy, this jack tore off the arm of a man who tried to get the animal to breed against its will. The victim was a friend of McVean and so the story was firmly marked in Bill's memory.

Not long after the news story, Bill received a carload of mares which he managed to sell, that is, all but one. This mare was old. No one wanted her no matter how low the price. Bill figured that the mare ought to be good for one more mule colt anyway.

Bill remembered the vicious jack and his good credentials for producing outstanding mules. He was in high demand no matter how high the danger. The owner often received a bonus for the jack's services.

Since it was getting toward the end of June and the end of the breeding season, Bill felt that the farmer would not object to having the jack impregnate one more mare. Bill took the half-dead mare to the farmer's place of business for one last fling of courtship.

However, when Bill arrived at the farm, no one greeted him. The farmer was nowhere to be seen. So Bill decided to go it alone. He figured he knew enough about breeding. The pen was surrounded by a plank fence, ten feet high. The mare was ambivalent. She didn't seem to want to be bred; on the other hand, she didn't refuse.

A huge gate led into the pen. On the gate, written in large letters, were explicit directions about opening the latch. "Raise up and shove forward toward Fortuna, drop down and shove toward Knobnoster, push toward Speed, and open." Bill followed the instructions to the letter and the latch opened. As he walked in, leading the mare, the gate closed behind him.

No sooner had the mare stepped into the lot, but a stud teaser poked his head out of a shed and began neighing loudly. This rejoicing aroused the prize jack and he immediately joined the chorus by braying. To add to the songfest, there was a little blue jack, not worth penning up, loose in the lot. Spotting the mare, the blue jack took off for her at breakneck speed. But the hand of man was against him. The last thing Bill wanted was a mule-colt from a no-account jack. He tried to ward off the blue jack and protect the mare. The blue jack refused to be warded off.

Then the prize jack entered the fray. Bill remembered the news story and it didn't seem so accidental now. Bill ran for the gate but it was barred and bolted. The directions were on the outside and Bill had forgotten the instructions, simple as they were. The plank fence was too high to climb and the jack was too big to subdue. He screamed for mercy and for help.

Luckily, the farmer heard the screaming, the neighing, the braying, and the sighing of the mare. He came dashing out of the farmhouse, picked up a two by four and managed to quiet the jacks.

The farmer turned on Bill: "What do you mean trying to do this yourself? And this fossilized mare to my outstanding jack? Don't you have any sense at all?"

Bill could only say: "The mare is truly no damn good, but I thought she could produce one more mule-colt."

Louis M. Monsees, the greatest jack breeder in Missouri, if not the whole world, lost his right forearm in a hunting accident with a shotgun. When asked by a stranger how he lost his forearm, Monsees always said it was done by an angry jack.

And then there was "Jackass Brown" down in Mississippi. Mr. Jim Brown was a rather well-to-do farmer who had been courtin' a certain lady in Memphis for many years. He had tried and tried to convince her that they should marry but she couldn't be convinced.

Finally, he decided that if he could just get her to come down to his farm she would be impressed enough so that a wedding could be planned. He implored and implored her. "I'll give you a standing invitation to come down and see me. When you are ready, I'll be ready. Just let me know."

Several weeks went by and no word. The widow woman was coy. Then one afternoon, Western Union called and said they had a wire for Mr. Brown. Farmer Brown had them read it to him over the phone: "Meet me at the depot at six. I'm ready."

It was Saturday afternoon and all the field hands had gone to town. Farmer Brown decided to hitch up a team himself. He started out to the pasture, but he couldn't get close to a horse. Every eligible animal, horse or mule, ran like a jackrabbit to avoid extra duty. Finally, he managed to trap a blind mule in a fence corner. He harnessed the blind mule to one side of the double-tree.

However, he still needed one more animal to make a team. Time was getting late. Town was a good two hour drive. In desperation, Brown spied a jackass securely enclosed in his pen. Brown decided to use the jack with the blind mule. The jack had other ideas. He thought he was going to the breeding pit since that was the usual course of events.

When taken out of the pen, he became excited and pranced around and around. Somehow Brown got the jack to the carriage. But the jack continued to prance and jump about. Brown used the whip. The jack and the mule went ten feet; then the jack had to prance some more. This went on for three or four times. Brown became exasperated. He picked up a board and hit the jack over the head. "Now listen you SOB! Who in hell got that telegram, you or me?"

As the story got out, Farmer Brown was forever known afterward as "Jackass Brown," even after the wedding.

Chapter Three

How to Recognize a Mule

A century ago most Americans knew what a mule was and looked like; some Missourians still do. Despite the effects of automation and more and more complex technology, the mule's long history and adaptability may guarantee him a place in the job market in the twenty first century. The mule numbers won't be as large as they were in 1900 and their tasks will be different. The mule will have to market his skills in a creative manner and he will have to become even more versatile and subject himself to periodic retraining.

Consequently, future employers need to be aware of the mule's distinguishing characteristics. They need to be sure that the mule has been manufactured correctly and has all the necessary parts properly arranged. Other animals have some of the mule's characteristics but not all of them and thus one has to be on guard to be sure of getting the real thing.

The mule's traits can be arranged in five categories: the ears; the bray; the kick; the curse; and the roll. All five characteristics are essential; leave one out and something else has become the subject matter.

The Ears

Some amateur geneticists have said that the mule must be a horse made by a bureaucracy since the mule just naturally looks funny. The most notorious single give-away sign of the mule is his ears. They have been described by Homer Croy, a popular Northwest Missouri writer, as "…those restless, flopping, sound catching, mood mirroring, jack-rabbit ears which quiver at the tips." In actuality, the jack-rabbit got his name from the fact that his ears were large like those of a jackass.

William Faulkner described the mule's ears as scissorlike. In silhouette, they do look like open scissors. However, because they were so long, it might have been more accurate to have said they were like hedge clippers.

The mules that were created after the Civil War, at the height of the "mule age," were black mules with extraordinarily large ears. If the ears were pushed down and sideways, they would measure almost 36 inches or a whole yardstick from tip to tip. Today's sorrel mule has big ears but not quite as big as those of the black mule.

Unquestionably, the extended size of the ear has caused the mule to be ridiculed without mercy. Jokes have abounded and parents have worried about the size and shape of their children's ears for fear they would resemble the mule. Roger Duty has written a popular children's book on donkey ears and the embarrassment they can cause.

One day the donkey became very self-conscious of his ears and wanted to go into permanent seclusion. A friendly dog advised him to wear his ears down like a cocker spaniel and then they wouldn't be so noticeable. A sheep counseled him to wear his ears pointed out to the side, as the sheep did. So was the style with goats and cows. A pig recommended that he wear his ears pointed forward, like the pig.

Finally, a wise sparrow taught the donkey some sound philosophy: "Donkey-donkey, silly donkey. You aren't a dog, You aren't a lamb. You aren't a pig. You are a donkey. Keep your ears up as donkeys do."

The next day, a little girl was walking in the country with her father when they happened upon the donkey. The little girl exclaimed: "Oh, Daddy! See the pretty donkey. His ears are so beautiful."

And that's the way mule showmen and breeders want the ears, tall and erect. They won't accept a floppy ear or ears too far back or forward. The ears should be a little thin but not too thin. There should also be a small tuft of hair at the tip to catch attention and to make the ear appear even longer than they are. "Lop-eared" is one of the strongest criticisms that a judge can aim at a mule or a human for that matter.

Since mule ears are so distinctive, they have gathered some interesting stories. One farmer, near Tipton, Missouri, was driving his mule home one evening. (The reader will have to determine if the farmer had been visiting the local tavern.) It was a summer night and, all at once, the farmer was astonished to see the ears of his mule light up and wonderous sparks shooting forth. Apparently, some fox fire had gotten on the mule's ears.

More frequent and more disturbing are the stories about the "haunt." When a mule started shying and acting more than commonly fractious, some people said there was a "haunt" present. The "haunt" could be seen by looking through the mule's ears. Needless to say, the "haunt" caused much fear and many superstitions. Others, trying to see a good side to the situation, said it was the "haunt" that gave the mule insight into forecasting weather and perceiving impending evils.

Finally, there should be some advice about touching a mule's ears. Don't do it unless one is looking for trouble.

The Bray

Human expression has been severely tested in trying to describe or reproduce the bray of a jackass or mule. Some observers have said that it was simply "tremendous"; others have called it "awful." It certainly was loud and could be terrifying. Scripture lovers compared the sound to the voice of a prophet crying in the wilderness.

Herodotus, the father of history, called attention to the significance of the bray in the Persian army's victory over the Scythians. The horses in the Scythian cavalry had never seen or heard a mule bray; so, when the Persian mules began their shouting in the battle, the Scythian horses were terrified and fled in disorder.

Greek poets compared the bray to the voice of Pericles which thundered and agitated all of Greece, so powerful was his eloquence. Like Pericles, the mule's voice was disproportionately loud and when the mule raised his voice, all opposition fell silent. The Greeks said that only crashing thunder could successfully compete for precedence with him.

Some farmers attested that one could hear a jack bray over three miles away. In the morning, the braying would start around four and there was no alarm more effective, not even the rooster.

Army veteran Maurice Ryan related an interesting incident about a proud mule in the Burma campaign during World War II. Ryan had become closely attached to Mule No. J704, starting with their training sessions in Fort Carson, Colorado. One day Ryan's unit was close by a fast flowing river in Burma where some natives were driving elephants across the river.

Ryan described it as follows: "...we watched them across there and they had elephants. And these elephant drivers or whatever you want to call them, and their dark skin—they were all natives—in that water. That elephant swimmin', you know, with that trunk up above. And he'd disappear, and the guy on his head would disappear, but pretty soon, they'd come back up and come across that river. But the funny part I wanted to tell you about, about this old Harry James (J704)....This elephant would trumpet, you know, and then this old mule would answer him. This old elephant would trumpet and this old mule would answer him, all the way through camp." This incident confirmed the name "Harry James," which had been given the mule at Fort Carson where he had outperformed all the other mules in his musical skill. He was also a good Democrat and he wasn't going to let the Republican elephant outdo him.

Fonnie L. Taylor, in Springfield, Missouri, told a story about another competition between jacks and turkeys. As a youngster, Fonnie went to his grandpa's farm where there were plenty of jacks and mules. The jacks had their own barn and outside there was a rail fence. "Sometimes there would be 200 turkeys sittin on the fence. Prettiest sight you ever seen and them old jacks'd bawl and then the turkeys'd gobbler. Hell, you never heard such a noise in that holler!"

Many farmers sold their mule colts about weaning time so that someone else could listen to the bawling and braying for the mother. Kalo Monsees said the noise was something unique. "They'd be missing the dams and shoot you couldn't hear a conversation anywhere near them. Much louder than a bunch of calves that are being weaned...just day and night."

Numerous observers have tried to describe the bray in words. Lydel Sims, who made a study of mule braying, said that the mule's bray was not what most people thought it was. Most farmers describe the bray with a hee-haw. Sims contended that it was really a "haw-hee". As a matter of fact, Sims stated that the bray began with a "wheeeeeehehehee" and then settled down to a haw-hee.

Avoiding these sound technicalities, Dr. J.E.V. Moore, a veterinarian in Hayti, Missouri, described the bray as similar to "...the sound of an alarm clock at five o'clock in the morning, the rushing through town of a freight train, a mother-in-law's condemning voice, a lover's whisper, the scream of a person falling out of a skyscraper, and the sound of sweet music as it comes from an organ."

A noted western writer, S.J. Barrows made these comments: "Sometimes the mule takes it into his head that he can sing. So long as he keeps this idea to himself nobody can complain. But the mule who has such a conceit is sure to publish it. One who has never heard a mule solo can form no idea of the rare cacophony it involves. No musical gamut can score it; no voice can imitate it. Only a mule can describe it. It is one of the grossest outrages on the public peace ever devised. Happy for the hearer if the bray be confined to one mule; but when two or three hundred happen to meet together and some base prompter among them says, 'Brethren, let us bray,' the antiphonal response, which is never refused, is perfectly overwhelming."

One unknown writer tried to capture the bray as follows:

"The burro raises his head skyward, without, however, raising his somnolent lids, his nostrils curl till his teeth show, and from his tautly opened mouth comes a long-drawn-out cry, a wild "Yah!" like the wail of a banshee, followed by three loud raspings and expiring in a series of wheezy throatings. Which done, the burro at once relapses into his former immobility. One takes the liberty to observe that the burro's voice is neither one of pain nor of poetry; it is one of exultation mixed with patronizing ridicule. A burro stands; he considers; he philosophizes; he attains Nirvana…."

William Faulkner said that the mule's "…voice is his own derision." Chesterton called it a "sickening cry." Mark Twain called attention to the fact that when the mule brays, he opens his mouth so wide that one could see right down to the works. The bray has earned all kinds of derisive names for the mule: Colorado Canary, Ozark Canary, Desert Canary, and Arizona Nightingale.

One Missouri cemetery had a burial plot for a family by the name of Bray. In the plot were four small markers for four small children. One marker was inscribed: "Will E. Bray." With no question mark.

There are many stories of church services being interrupted, if not terminated, by the bray of the mules outside. A Reverend Mr. Darley told of one such incident: "One Sabbath evening a burro (Maud) was hitched to a post near the back window of the church. As I commenced preaching, she began braying. First a solo, low, clear, penetrating, not altogether unmusical; then a kind of duet, the outgoing breath making one sort of noise, the incoming another. This was followed by a quartet of noises. The burros of the neighborhood began answering, and I really think from the way Maud then let out, she thought it was an encore."

Not only did the bray interrupt church services, but, on one occasion, it caused a newly married couple to separate and end their marriage. The groom had a long established habit of rising early, making a cup of coffee, and going out on the porch where he brayed back and forth with his mule. When he brought his new bride to his cottage and continued his early dialogue with his mule, the new wife walked out.

One gold miner testified that a burro's braying saved the man's life. "You see the gulch was very narrow, with steep banks on either side. We had a cloudburst. Such rain, great Caesar! It came down in torrents, it fairly spilled over; it was more like a deluge than an ordinary rainstorm. I was curled up in my tent with Jerry, my dog, and trying to keep dry when all of sudden, that old burro ran up to the tent and began to bray....The water was then close to the tent. I had no time to lose, so I rose quickly, pulled the pickets and got to a place of safety....If not for the old burro, I might have been a goner." (Harold H. Dunham)

A glorious conclusion to the jack's braying involved Immaculate Conception Abbey in northwest Missouri. Periodically, the Abbey rented some pasture to Leo Baumli for his jacks and mules. They adjusted to the Benedictine regimen rather easily. St. Benedict had given his monks two commandments to guide their monastic life: Ora et Labora—Pray and Work. One can see that the ora is contained in the labora; in the same way, one's work should be included in one's prayer of praise to God. Over the centuries, the mule has shown his affinity to work and doing it in a good spirit.

Moreover, the Benedictines gather frequently every day for prayer in choir. One could hear often the latin word, Oremus—let us pray. The jacks would say: Bremus—let us bray. Their chant did not follow the rules and customs of Solesmes, but their braying certainly caught the attention of the monks and, probably, of God too.

Finally, St. Benedict had emphasized the virtue of humility as the key to achieving sanctity and perfection in this life of trial. The mule had learned these precepts of wisdom to the twelfth degree over the centuries, more or less in the way Benedict instructed.

The Curse

Maybe mules curse. It is unlikely since cursing is said to be the habit of limited minds. Some have explained the sad look upon the face of a mule by the fact that his big ears picked up very acutely all the cursing that occured about him. There seemed to be no concern for his hypersensitivity.

No matter, mules have an innate ability in causing the loss of temper by those who were supposed to be their superiors. Somehow when the mule was around, things did not go as planned. The resulting frustration provided the perfect opportunity to develop the art of cursing.

Some expert mulemen, such as General George Crook, thought cursing was completely the wrong way to deal with this frustration and the mule. He believed that a mule refused to act as ordered because something was wrong. The handler should carefully reconsider the situation from every angle to determine what was causing the mule to disobey. With pack mules, it was often the case that the cargo was improperly loaded. With wagon mules, it was often a misaligned harness which was causing mule's flesh to be rubbed raw. Or, in both cases, the muleskinner was trying to force the mule to enter a dangerous situation.

No matter how high the prestige and wisdom of General Crook, most mule drivers and handlers were frequent and expert swearers. They argued that cursing was instinctual. Since some people have better instincts than others, these sensitive leaders became muleteers.

Moreover, the cursers argued it was unhealthy to conceal and suppress anger or frustration. In such situations, even Shakespeare said "…abstinence engenders maladies." The mule handler thought that swearing unclogged the heart and got rid of unhealthy vapors in the blood. Today, they would say it reduces cholesterol. Earlier in this century, a noted medical expert, W. N. P. Barbellion stated that "…swearing is like pimples, better to come out, cleanses the moral system. The person who controls himself must have lots of terrible oaths circulating in his blood." Consequently, cursing was part of nature's way of staying healthy.

Other muleskinners argued that plain, ordinary talking to the mules had no effect. Even eloquent speech. Thus they had to resort to more "vivid" language and develop a high level skill in cursing. Some may have reached the heights of Ovid, to whom Ashley Montagu, a professional student of the history of cursing, attributed the most excellent piece of literary cursing. One of Ovid's characters let go a blast that lasted for six hundred verses, a classic vituperative explosion. It contained all the basic elements of good cursing: expletives, maledictions, adjurations, objurgations, and abusives.

Because some muleskinners cursed so magnificently, one could wonder where they learned their trade. They knew how to curse by all the gods: Zeus, Jupiter, Mars, Apollo, Hercules, Dionysos, Poseidon, Demeter, Minerva, Juno, Venus and many others. They knew how to invoke every conceivable pain down upon their victim: hunger, sleeplessness, impotency, mental anguish, poverty, to name a few.

A good cursing also included death: death by drowning, by fire, by torture, by sword, by hanging, by poison, by choking, and by any and every mean circumstance imaginable.

Some of the muleskinners would even use the most dreadful of all curses, the Sedgwick curse: "May the great fiend, booted and spurred, with a sythe in his girdle, ride headlong down your throat."

Montagu commented that the coming of the gasoline engine removed "...the living spur (often the mule) to expressive, non-blasphemous profanity...." The men whose lives were bound to beasts of burden, the cavalry man, the artillery man, but most of all, the muleskinner, had raised "the poor man's poetry" to a noble and high art form. Mechanized equipment can fail but the reaction to such failure had a different character which somehow was less colorful and imaginative.

Though it is difficult to imagine, some people continued to regard cursing as unnecessary and unacceptable, even people with esteemed reputations. During the Revolutionary War, George Washington became so disturbed by the prevalence and vehemence of the cursing that he issued the following order:

> The General is sorry to be informed that the
> foolish and wicked practice of profane cursing
> and swearing, a vice heretofore little known in
> an American army, is growing into fashion. He
> hopes the officers will, by example as well as
> influence, endeavor to check it, and that both
> they and the men will reflect, that we can have
> little hope of the blessing of heaven on our
> arms, if we insult it by our impiety and folly.
> Added to this, it is a vice so mean and low,
> without any temptation, that every man of sense
> and character detests and despises it.

Despite this denunciation, some biographers of Washington have noted that the General was known to swear, rather vehemently, when the occasion demanded it. The historians do not record whether mules may have caused his outbursts.

General Ulysses Grant once said: "I am not aware of ever having used a profane expletive in my life, but I would have the charity to excuse those who may have done so if they were in charge of a train of Mexican pack-mules at the time."

Mark Twain's wife was often angered by her husband's prolonged swearing. In an attempt to make him reconsider this vile habit, one day she let him have a long and bitter attack which ran through the whole gamut of the cursing registry. At the end of her explosion, Twain smiled and said: "You have all the words right, but you don't have the melody."

During World War I, a young man by the name of Homer Larson joined the army. He had just graduated from the University of Virginia with a major in Greek. Eventually he was assigned to an artillery transport unit in Europe. The conditions of mud, rough terrain, pernicious enemy, and mules were perfect for an unending barrage of profanities. However, the sick and dying found such tirades very disquieting as they prepared themselves for the hereafter.

Homer Larson wanted to give comfort to the disquieted, but not interfere with the successful conduct of the war. Somehow, by the grace of God, he decided to substitute short Greek words for the good, old-fashioned, Anglo-Saxon four letter words. He recalled distinctly his opening day in "Freshman Greek," when an anemic looking professor recited the ancient alphabet with a dramatic flourish. At the time, Homer thought it had the same sound and cadence of good cursing.

The major problem for Homer was how was he going to teach Greek to these Army muleskinners. With great persistence and good humor, he tried his experiment. The mules and men responded haltingly, but eventually they were chanting Greek cadences and the mules were stepping out in a lively manner.

In a tight situation, the driver would scream: Alpha, Beta, Omega Zeus! Nu, Kappa, Psi! The mules seemed to cooperate and Homer Larson had found a justification for majoring in Greek.

Of course, some of the men lapsed from time to time into their own authentic profanity. A lanky lad from Appalachia would whine a nasal muledictory: "Lambda, Alpha Chi, you low down bloody varmit."

Or a stocky German-American would sputter: "Zeta Tau Pi, Gott dam you!"

Josh Billings called the mule a stubborn fact. How in the world could one make him follow orders when he was not so inclined. One could hit him with a club or whip, but one needed a tremendous propulsive force to do it successfully. This force, oftentimes, was an unlimited stock of profanity which the driver hurled into the sensitive "ears" of the mule.

Josh once heard of a theoretical strategy that could have won the Civil War for the North much more quickly. If all the mule drivers of the Army of the Potomac had been put in the trenches around Richmond, then, when the enemy advanced within earshot, at a given signal, these drivers would start swearing simultaneously. The Rebs would have either thrown down their arms and surrendered, or fled into the vastness of the Blue Ridge.

Today, with the mule playing such a small part in the lives of many people, some scholars greatly fear for the future of profanity. Today's swearing is so repetitive, lacks imagination, and has no euphony and little alliteration. Montagu suggested the establishment of a new foundation, like the National Science Foundation or the National Endowment for the Arts, to encourage some roiling new phrases like G. B. Shaw's "thirty thousand thunders."

The Kick

Unquestionably, the mule's kick made a deep impression because everyone who has ever dealt with mules will quickly mention being kicked as one of the memorable aspects of the relationship. An Ozarkian once described the mule's kick as follows: "the action and force of a piston with the accuracy and enthusiasm of a ballet dancer."

Josh Billings said that the main things which made a mule so highly respectable were the great accuracy and speed of his kicking. This astute observer of western life said that the mule was a sure-footed animal, so sure-footed that he had seen a mule kick a man standing fifteen feet off ten times in a second. Josh continued his praise:

> "Unquestionably he had no equal in this field
> of amusement. His legs are small, his feet were
> small, but his ambition in this direction was
> large. He could kick with wonderful accuracy.

Muledrivers tell me he could kick a fly off his
ear, with unerring accuracy. This being so,
larger objects were never missed when they were
within range. And the distance included within
the mule's range was simply incredible."

A famous verse helped explain how the mule used his feet:

On a mule you find two feet behind
Two feet you find before
You stand behind before you find
What the two behind be for.

Once there was a popular song in Missouri by the name of "Whoa
Mule Whoa." The last verses went as follows:

I took my gal out for a ride
The mule began to buck
He threw her off onto the ground
And spoiled her Sunday smock.
My girl swore that she'd have revenge
And stooped to get a stick.
The mule let go with both hind legs
And laid my girl out slick.

I took her upon my back
And laid her in the bed.
I put a plaster on her feet
And one upon her head.
The doctor came and felt her pulse,
Pronounced her very low.
And all you could hear that poor girl say was,
Whoa Mule Whoa.

Missourians often said that a mule could kick one into next week
or even into next year. Strangely, many farmers blamed themselves for
getting kicked. They apologized for the mule by saying they got too
close when the mules were playing, or they had surprised the mule.
R. Kohl, a highly respected Missouri mule man admitted that he had
been kicked in the chest and knocked out. "But it was my fault. I ran
up to scare him and got too close." Some farmers said that a baby
could crawl around the feet of a mule all day and not get kicked. But
mothers didn't particularly want to test the theory.

Once a farmer boasted that his mule never kicked. To prove it to the jeering bystanders, he took a chicken feather and tickled the mule's heels. Two days later, the preacher said at the funeral that it was a case of misplaced confidence.

There was a sad incident one day in the heart of the Ozark Mountains. A mule kicked a farmer's mother-in-law to death. A tremendous crowd turned out for the funeral, but it was made up almost entirely by men. The minister commented, "This old lady must have been mighty popular because so many people have left their work to come to her funeral."

"They're not here for the funeral," said the farmer. "They're here to buy my mule."

President Lincoln told this kicking story. One hot day he was riding a mule and the flies were bothering the mule no end. So the mule was kicking and swishing, trying to scare off the flies. Finally, he kicked so high that he got his foot caught in the stirrup. Lincoln turned to the mule and said: "If you're going to get up and ride, I'll get down and walk."

Once an insurance agent approached a farmer about buying some insurance. He asked the farmer if had ever had an accident. The farmer replied: "Wal no. A mule kicked in two of my ribs once, and a rattlesnake bit me on the leg a couple of weeks ago." "Great Scott!" said the agent, "Don't you consider those accidents?" "Wal, no sir. They done it on purpose."

Missourians have always said that a mule will love you for 25 years just to get the chance to kick you. The Greeks warned that a mule makes seven attempts (one source says every day) to kick and kill his master. Negro farmers said that the mule had so much goodness in his face, that he don't have none left for his hind legs.

The railroad companies had learned to respect the mule's kick the hard way. After so many shipping cars had been demolished, the companies made a law that no mule could be shipped with its shoes on. Mules were bad enough shoeless, but, with shoes, they were capable of destroying just about anything.

Sometimes they even waited longer than the prescribed 25 years. One famous story involved a wealthy Missouri farmer who had a mule by the name of Sidney. Sidney was a remarkable mule who lived to the mystical age of 33. To commemorate the mule in a fitting manner, the farmer dried Sidney's skull in the sun and then hung it on his front porch for all to see. Beneath the skull, he inscribed these words:

"Here hangs Sidney, the mule who could do no wrong."

For many years, the mule's head hung in this place of honor. In the summer months, the farmer would often take a siesta on the porch in a hammock under the skull. One day, as the farmer was sleeping, a wind knocked the skull down and it fell on the farmer's head, killing him instantly.

One of the workmen, after the tragedy, said that he had tried to warn the farmer that he should never trust that mule, even when it was dead and partly gone. The mule is just a contrary so and so who will get you one way or another, sooner or later, even after they are dead.

Mark Twain said that if he were ever asked to give an oration for a dead mule, he would make sure that he was allowed to stand by the head of the mule, the only safe place. Even dead mules are dangerous as Sidney illustrated.

On another occasion, in a small Ozark town, a mule died on the street. The funeral director was called to remove the body. After a great deal of effort in loading the carcass into a wagon, the director proceeded to remove the mule outside of town. At one place, the wagon wheel hit a deep mud-hole and jarred the mule's body. The jar caused the hind legs to kick out in a spontaneous reaction which knocked the director clear off the wagon.

Thus the ole Missouri rule: Never position yourself behind or in range of a mule's hind legs. Another saying holds: A Missouri mule kicks by no rules. One keen observer noted that after a mule was broken, there is still a crook in his leg and only waiting to kick you.

And they can kick from any angle. Some people have sworn that they were standing in front of a mule and the mule was still able to kick them. Feral Egan told the story of a muleskinner and the artful kicking of a mule. A vaquero was trying to manage a particularly bad critter, "holding him by the head and leaning over to pick up his lariat, when the mule surprised him with a stunner." It nearly knocked him unconscious. "For the life of me, I could not see how it was done. But the boys said he did it fairly and I was not entitled to claim a 'foul'."

Some mules liked to strike with their front feet as well as kick with their the hind legs. As some Missouri farmers learned: "Watch both ends. Because both ends work!"

With all that power in a mule's legs, imagine the danger in shoe-ing a mule? Blacksmiths had two methods which they found successful even though they were highly stressful. Method One called for the mule to be slung up in the air like an oxen and then to strap his feet. The second method consisted of walking the mule into a noose and then casting him to the ground by drawing his legs together. In each case, the mule would struggle violently. God help the blacksmith who made a mistake in his methodology.

Probably the most famous story about the kick of a mule was written by Alphonse Daudet and is entitled: "The Pope's Mule." It so happened that while the Popes were in exile in Avignon, one of the Popes, Pope Boniface, had a mule for which he had a great affection. There was nothing that the Pope withheld from the mule if he thought it would give the mule delight. This rule even applied to the Pope's favorite wine, Chateau Neuf des Papes.

One day, while the Pope was riding the mule, a young fellow, named Tistet, approached and heaped praise and affection upon the mule. Of course the Pope admired Tistet for his kindness and admiration of the mule. Tistet repeated this attention day after day, and won the Pope's trust and favor. Promotion followed promotion for Tistet which was due completely to his care of the mule. Gradually, the Pope turned over to Tistet all aspects of caring for the mule.

It turned out that Tistet had no affection whatsoever for the mule. He had simply exploited the mule's relation to the Pope to win high positions and access to a very comfortable life. Tistet began to make life miserable for the mule whenever the Pope was out of sight. There seemed no end to the villainous tricks and cruelty devised by Tistet.

Gradually, the mule developed a great lust for the opportunity to kick Tistet. At this point, the Pope sent Tistet to Naples on a special diplomatic mission. This assignment consumed seven years which were a wonderful time of merriment for Tistet.

When Tistet finally returned to Avignon, the Pope arranged a special celebration. The mule heard of the upcoming feast and she began to practice her heels on the wall behind her.

As Tistet approached the Pope to receive the new insignia, the magnificent Provencal paused to give the mule a friendly pat, making sure that the Pope was watching. The positioning was just right. The mule let go with both her heels.

"There, take it, villain! Seven years have I kept it for thee!"

And she gave him so terrible a kick, so terrible that even at nearby Pamperigouste the smoke was seen, a whirlwind of blond dust, in which flew the feathers of an ibis, and that was all that remained of the unfortunate Tistet.

In France, there is an old proverb: "That fellow! Distrust him! He's like the Pope's mule who kept her kick for seven years."

Finally, Carl Sandberg told the story of a Missouri mule "who took aim with his heels at an automobile rattling by. The car turned a somersault, hit a fence, ran right along through a cornfield till it came to a gate, moved onto the road, and went its way as though nothing had happened. The mule heehawed with desolation: "What's the use?"

Surely the kick of a mule had only the superlative degree. There was no positive or comparative. Marion T. Reed believed that one could've locked his mule up in a bank vault and he would have kicked his way out.

The Roll

It wasn't "Rock and Roll," but the mule has been a long time advocate of "rolling." It had nothing to do with the "Holy Rollers," although the mule's rolling was a whole commitment. Horses and other animals roll too, but none do it with the relish and enthusiasm of the mule.

At the end of a hard day's work or a long march, the mule loved to get down and roll. They appeared so tired that one expected them to just collapse when unharnessed or unloaded. Somehow there was a hidden reservoir of energy to allow this highly kinetic exercise. Some farmers would even prepare a corner of the barnyard with "clean" and fine-textured dirt, or with sand, for the mules to roll in.

Harold O. Weight argued that mules curried themselves by rolling on the ground with "cyclonic vigor." He added "that the cloud of dust raised was suggestive of a Death Valley sandstorm." James W. Stoole added that it was a "mule's luxury to roll—not onesidedly and lazily, but in a regular tumble, accompanied by snorts, groans, and grunts. Every time his pack is removed, he is sure to engage in a general shaking up of his whole corporal system." What a sight to see 200 mules rolling vigorously at one time.

Some traders would determine the value of the mule by the vigor with which it rolled. One roll meant the mule was worth a hundred dollars. Two rolls meant two hundred; three rolls meant three hundred and on up the ladder.

The mule expert, Melvin Bradley, was of the opinion that rolling was associated with the sensitive skin of the mule. The mule can hardly tolerate a fly or mosquito to land on him. And yet their skin is very tough.

J. Olen White told about his jack who insisted on rolling two or three times before he would breed a mare. "My friends thought I was storyin' to 'em, but they had to see it 'fore they'd believe it. Every jack has a little somethin' different."

A popular manual circulated by the Horse and Mule Association of America described the mule's propensity to roll in this manner: "It is common practice in the south to pull the harness off mules at noon or night, and turn them loose in a big corral or lot with access to all the water, hay and grain they want. They usually will first roll in a sand pile, which should be available." Only then will they go about eating and drinking.

Thus the mule handlers would say: "A roll is as good as a feed", or, "You let a mule roll, he's good for another day's work."

With these five characteristics in mind, one should be capable of recognizing a mule when the occasion arises. However, there are forces at work which try to confuse the public and make the task quite difficult. Most of these forces are political as one might imagine. Democrats are harder and harder to define and identify. President Clinton has talked about being a "New Democrat", but he has serious trouble in explaining what he meant by the new name.

Political cartoonists, such as Engelhardt of the *St. Louis Post Dispatch* have distorted the image of the donkey at times by attaching an elephant trunk onto its nose. They do this to illustrate the difficulty that exists in distinguishing a Democrat from a Republican in today's world. Further comment is needed here which leads into The Mule and Politics.

─── Chapter Four ───

The Mule and Politics

The mule and politics have mixed throughout American History to produce an enduring system, some for the good, and some for the bad. What politician, voter, political scientist, political analyst, journalist, pollster, television anchor or historian has not been called a "jackass" many times over? It just happens inevitably in the melee of politics. Winston Churchill saw the connection between the mule and politics vividly. As a young man he had been bucked off rather embarrassingly by a mule. He said it was his first experience in politics.

In 1992, George Bush made a fatal political mistake when he called William Clinton, his opponent, a "bozo." Using this new name reflected more on Bush and how he was faring in the campaign than on Clinton. Bush should have called Clinton a "jackass," and everyone would have had a good laugh. Clinton and the Democrats would have had no complaints because of their party's symbol. Bush's use of a new idiom hurt him. He should have remembered his successful use in 1984 of the phrase: "I kicked a little ass tonight." Maybe, as President, he felt it improper to use such mulish language.

The mule represents the pragmatic and get-things-done attitude of Americans. It shies away from the abstractions of politics: liberty, justice, law, liberalism, conservatism and democracy. The mule pulls, works and rolls in the mire and mud of everyday nitty-gritty politiking. Who is to say which part is more important?

The mule's role has had several parts to it. Often he represented the common people and the working classes. This role is easy to understand since the mule has been assigned consistently the menial and backbreaking work. Although much of American ideology has extolled the significance and centrality of government of, by and for the people, the reality in many times and places would attest to the neglect and abuse of the average American. The mule provided a fitting image of this neglect and abuse.

In sharp contrast to this role, politicians on the way up the political ladder often attack the power figures and leaders in the opposing party or in their own party by calling them mules. In his campaign for governor of Alabama, Jim Folsum dramatized his role against wealth and predatory interests by attacking the Big Mules of Birmingham. He thereby affirmed an earlier protest movement against the "big mules and those that got-rocks."

Caroline H. Keith, author of a recent biography of Maryland senator, Millard E. Tydings, called Tydings one of the "Big Mules" in the Senate. She quoted Lister Hill, a fellow Democrat and senator, who extolled Tydings as a veteran leader to whom newcomers looked for guidance. Richard Rovere called Tydings a "titan of the Senate," and a "powerhouse." Keith said that Tydings came from nowhere, fought his way up from nothing, ascended through sheer strength of character, intelligence and boundless self-confidence to gain the inner sanctum, the circle of men who ran the U.S. Senate. Here the appellation of "mule" is clearly one of admiration and esteem.

These uses of "mule' contrast sharply with the frequently employed image of the mule for the lowly, the outcast, the poor and disfranchised citizenry. At the death of Martin Luther King Jr., the mules pulling his coffin were a powerful symbol of his fight for the poor of America. Shortly after his funeral, there was a Poverty March on Washington, and again, the fifteen mule-drawn wagons enunciated powerfully the message and purpose for that march.

In yet another way, the mule, or more accurately, his papa, the jackass, has provided the means to ridicule politicians, their foibles, and their misuse of the political process. This function can be judged as one of the factors that has saved the American political system. Without humor and ridicule, some politicians may have ruined the country long ago with their conceit, pomposity and self-aggrandizement.

For example, Mark Twain once defined a senator as a person who makes laws when he is not doing time. On another occasion, he said that he had a mule who would kick up his heels when Twain told him a joke. Once Twain introduced the mule to a politician and the mule kicked the barn down in laughter.

Mark Twain also liked to ask a friend: Did you ever try to make yourself believe a lie? The answer: Yes, when I try to convince myself that certain politicians were honest.

As the years go by, politicians continue their comedy. Senator Max Baucus recently became angry over criticism which said that

President Clinton's trade policy was confused. Baucus retaliated: "Let's applaud our President for being clever. *The Wall Street Journal* would criticize him for taking unpredictable 'zigzags' in trade negotiations. But do we want to be predictable as we sit down to negotiate with our trading partners?"

One commentator, Irving Silverstein, described it as follows: "A successful politician is a model of adaptability. He can talk out of both sides of his mouth and off the top of his head and keep his ear to the ground."

Once a mule farmer was asked his opinion of ticks, those repulsive, bloodsucking arachnids. Which ticks caused him, his family and his animals the most trouble? After a little recollection and head scratching, the farmer replied that the answer was really quite simple: "It had to be those poliTICS."

Lyndon B. Johnson had to endure considerable derision because of his policies and personality. Victor Navasky believed that "sacred cows" are for milking humor. So he and his friends devised a story about the "animal ranch" and ridiculed LBJ's "Grade A Society At the end of the story, the band played the bull's campaign song (by Julia Ward Cow).

The song consisted of Hee haw and Haw hee, one after another in both the verses and the chorus and was entitled: The Cattle Hymn of the Republic.

Some students of American culture maintain that Americans have a fixation on two things, sex and politics. It is interesting that the jackass or ass has played a significant part in both of these fixations. The double meaning has been used in so many different ways that an observer has to wonder at the imagination's power of creativity and/or depravity. Just when one thinks every variation possible has been heard, up pops a new one. Carter tried a new slant with the "rabbit" in one of his strategies. But he redeemed himself by raising the question of "lust" in the heart.

In light of this history, it is interesting that one of the major political parties has the donkey or jackass as its symbol. Shortly after the Civil War, a cartoonist portrayed Horace Greeley, the Democratic presidential hopeful, in a quandary, being pulled in opposite directions by the contrary mules in his party.

A few years later, Ignatius Donnelly characterized the Democrats as being mule-like, "without pride of ancestry or hope of posterity." However, it was the famous cartoonist, Thomas Nast, who firmly united the Democratic Party with the donkey. In 1870, he drew a cartoon entitled: "A Live Jackass Kicking a Dead Lion." The "Jackass" stood for the Copperhead Press, and the "Lion" referred to Edwin M. Stanton. This cartoon is now remembered as the earliest use of the donkey to symbolize Democratic feeling. Ever after, it has been the symbol of the Democratic Party, and Democrats have taken pride in the emblem.

Many examples could be found similar to the following: in 1956 Representative Dunklin of Dade County, Missouri, took the speaker's rostrum in the Missouri House of Representatives and said: "A true Democrat is a hard-headed mule. Don't think he isn't. He don't want anybody dictatin' to him."

When James (Jim) Reed ran for the United States Senate in 1922, he ran single handed. Reed, the Senate's "Greatest Belligerent," had been read out of the Democratic Party and was opposed by the Anti-Saloon League, the Ku Klux Klan, and most other groups. Even the ailing Woodrow Wilson rose from his sick bed and intervened in the election against Reed.

Reed's victory in the election was unparalleled and unexpected. *The Birmingham News* came up with the explanation: "…maybe they vote the mules up there." Actually only mules and Missourians would have voted for Jim Reed in 1922.

During several elections this century, both parties have resorted to staging races or other contests between donkeys and elephants to arouse voter interest. In 1988, Boston brought the two animals together in the downtown district to remind people to vote. It turned out to be a very peaceful, uneventful affair.

Sometimes the confrontation was not so peaceful. In 1956, in Sandy Spring, Maryland, some Republican women arranged a funding to be attended by an elephant and a donkey. The donkey, nick-named Adlai Stevenson, really kicked up his heels. He ate one of the floral wreaths, kicked the hostess, and knocked her dog unconscious for barking at his heels. The elephant was "placid" while the donkey stole the show.

Political observers have smiled at the recent phenomenon of both political parties vying with each other in their adulation of Harry S. Truman. In 1992, even the third party candidate, Ross Perot, tried to get on Truman's coattails. Articles by political pundits argued how well Perot fit the Truman image. Some even went so far as to admit that Perot had the ears of a Democratic jackass.

41

While Truman was president, both parties had a strong tendency to wish that he would go away. Now, the evaluation of Truman's presidency is exalted and it is bi-partisan. The same phenomenon has occurred in relation to the mule. Both parties do not hesitate to invoke the mule to strengthen their positions. In 1956, William Spiced, running for Congress in the Third Arkansas District, made a fealty trip to Washington to call on President Eisenhower. After candidate Spiced had chatted with the President, he remarked to newsmen how well the Chief Executive looked following his recent illness: "To me he looks as tough as an Arkansas mule. I thought he looked wonderful." Three days later, a wire report noted that Adlai E. Stevenson, still desirous of the presidency, had the constitution of an "Illinois plow mule."

Throughout his political career, Truman drew upon his relationships with the mule to advance his cause. He had farmed with mules and had spent "many hours in the field looking at the south end of a mule going north." Almost every farmer had used that expression many times over. Truman's ability to control and handle mules certainly helped him become an officer in the Army in World War I. One of his favorite photographs showed him at the Missouri State Fair with two champion mules. Truman loved to point to the picture and say: By the way, I'm the one on the left.

As most Americans know, Truman loved to take a vigorous walk in the morning before confronting the problems in the White House. Before retiring in the evening, he would have an aide call the weather bureau to check on the upcoming weather. One evening, the aide reported that the morrow would be a beautiful and sunny day, just perfect for his daily constitutional. So Truman was up bright and early. He had proceeded only a few yards toward the Washington Monument, when he saw a farmer being pulled in a wagon by a mule. The farmer had a big umbrella over his head. Truman laughed at the farmer and asked why he had the umbrella up. The farmer told the president in no uncertain terms that it was going to rain in a few minutes and the President would be soaked to the skin before he could get back to the White House. Truman told him that he was crazy.

But sure enough, within a few minutes, it poured down rain in great quantities, and Truman was soaked. When he got back to the White House, he directed an aide to go out and find that farmer. After a long search, the aide found the farmer and brought him to the oval office. The smiling Truman asked the farmer how he knew it was going to rain, when the "experts" didn't. The farmer replied that the answer was easy, it was his mule. Truman then wanted to know more. The farmer continued, when it is going to be a clear, sunny day, the mule's ears point straight up. When it is going to rain or storm, his ears are flat down on his neck. When the farmer saw Truman, the mule's ears were flat on his neck and the farmer knew for sure it would rain right away.

Truman laughed and laughed, picked up the phone and fired the head of the weather service. The President then made the farmer and his mule the new head. And you know what? Ever since every jackass in the country has gone to Washington looking for a job.

The average person liked the above story because it helped him understand how so many jackasses held positions in the Washington bureaucracy. Truman, himself, wondered which jackass was responsible for naming the department in charge of all the outdoors, the Department of the Interior.

Mules and Truman fit together in all kinds of ways. When Truman talked tough to the Russians, news commentators reminded Americans that the Missourian was speaking in the muleskinner's fashion. When Truman's detractors spoke, they usually referred to the less pleasant characteristics of the mule and his paternal ancestry. He was stubborn, foolish and stupid. He simply was incapable of performing the job which he had inherited from Roosevelt.

When Truman was inaugurated in 1949, a prominent place in his parade went to a special team of sorrel mules from Lamar, Missouri, Truman's birthplace. Earlier, another famous and powerful political figure from Missouri, Champ Clark, drove a beautiful team of mules in a special parade to honor his selection as Speaker of the House. The names of the two mules were poetic, The Belle of Pike and The Belle of Callaway. Pike County has been prominent in Western History and it was Clark's home county.

Once there was another mule that wanted to star in a presidential inaugural. Her name was Maude and her owner was W. R. Berridge of Kentucky. Berridge strongly endorsed William Jennings Bryan in the 1896 campaign and thought Bryan would win. He prepared Maude for the festivities. But Bryan lost. The ritual was reenacted in 1900, but Bryan lost again to William McKinley. In 1904, Bryan did not win the Democratic nomination, but, in 1908, he ran for the third time. Berridge thought for sure that Bryan would make it this time. Besides Maude was getting along in years; she was now 35. Bryan lost again.

In Wilson's administration, the Golden Orator became Secretary of State, but many realized that Bryan's dream of being president would never come true. Maude realized it too. Her dream would be unfulfilled too. Berridge did provide a splendid funeral for Maude and a large tombstone was erected over her grave.

It read: "Here Lies Maude. She is Gone But Not Forgotten." A Louisville editor noted; it is better to be gone and not forgotten, than to be forgotten and not gone. The editor was pointing to Bryan in the waning years of his life.

When Champ Clark was serving his last term as Speaker of the House, he had the occasion to meet Sam Rayburn in St. Louis on their way back to Washington. (In 1912, Woodrow Wilson became the Democratic candidate for President and won the election over the encumbent, Taft, and the Progressive Party candidate, Theodore Roosevelt. In the Democratic Convention that year, Wilson and Champ Clark had an exciting and drawn out struggle for the nomination with Wilson finally winning. Clark had come very close.)

Getting back to the story, Clark and Rayburn were sitting together in a Pullman Coach as the train pulled out of St. Louis. As they were talking, Rayburn looked out the window and saw a large number of Missouri mules being driven into a pen. Nudging Clark, Sam pointed out the window and said: "Look, Champ, thar go some of your constituents."

"Yep," said Champ, never beaten in a verbal draw, "Thar they go. They're going down to Austin to take their seats in the Texas Legislature and to teach school."

Another Champ Clark mule story is found in Ambrose Bierces' *Devil's Dictionary*. Bierce regarded the anecdote so highly, he used it as an illustration and definition of the word "story."

One time Clark was home to visit his congressional district and he rode into the village of Jebique, Missouri. He stopped at a favorite saloon and the boys decided to pull a prank on the renowned Congressman. They told Champ that it was most unkind to leave his mule out in the hot sun. Surely it would roast in such heat. Clark paid no attention and said the mule was tough and could handle it.

The day before Clark arrived, a fire had destroyed a barn and several horses. The conspirators led Clark's mule away and replaced it with the charred remains of a horse. Then they told Clark that he had to do something because the mule was beginning to smell. Clark simply replied that his mule had the best nose in the county.

Eventually Clark ambled outside but said nothing when he saw the supposed remains of his mule. He simply started to walk home. Outside of town, as he walked by a field in the moonlight, he saw his mule standing by the fence. Now Clark was frightened and he rushed back into town and stayed in the hotel for the night.

Clark had a number of adulterated versions of this story's ending. One version had Clark coming out of the saloon, and, upon seeing the burned remains, he lifted his eyes toward the sun and said: "Gentlemen, indeed, I did not realize that it was that hot."

Another Pike County contribution to Missouri politics was the phrase: "Gone up Salt River." It seemed that a certain man named Jackson had a great desire to serve in some political office. He conducted a strenuous campaign but was defeated, which embarrassed him greatly. He moved his family from Louisiana, Missouri, to the nearby mouth of the Salt River. Friends wondered where he had gone. Others replied that he had gone up Salt River.

In the next election, Jackson tried again to be elected. Again he was defeated. He moved farther up the river. By this time, Jackson's habit of moving up Salt River appealed to people's sense of humor and even the newspapers got wind of the story. It became a standing joke all over the country for defeated politicians. "Why he's gone up Salt River." (Mrs. Gaylord O'Conner)

The mule could also be used to teach a young legislator a lesson. Representative Joe Blout was in his first days in the Missouri legislature, fresh out of the Ozarks. When the Appropriation Committee reported out a fifty million dollar bill and the House quickly passed the measure with an overwhelming vote, Representative Blout thought it would be even easier to get his first bill passed. It was a private claims bill on behalf of a constituent who wanted damages for his dead mule. There had been a contest between the mule and a state highway department truck and the mule had lost. The mule was valued at $250. Like all dead mules killed as a result of negligence on the part of the government, this one was a thoroughbred. Representative Blout introduced a bill to compensate the farmer $250 for his dead mule.

Much to his surprise, the Assembly proceeded to debate at great length the pros and cons of the dead mule case. This was in striking contrast to the facility and rapidity with which the fifty million dollar appropriation bill had been passed the previous day. The debate became acrimonious and lasted a full week. Finally, it come to a vote and was defeated 110 to 1. Blout cast the one favorable vote. Immediately, he sought out a wise and veteran legislator and asked: "Charlie, what happened?"

Charlie innocently replied: "What do you mean?"

Representative Blout then explained, "I can't understand how a fifty million dollar appropriation bill could be passed so quickly and easily with so little debate, and my $250 mule bill was debated all week and then was defeated."

"Oh, that's easy," said Charlie. "Everybody knows all about a $250 mule, but nobody knows a single damn thing about a fifty million dollar appropriation bill."

Probably no other Missourian won more honors for his blue-ribbon mules than mule raiser and trader, Ed Frazier. He had so many trophies that there was talk of banning him and his mules from further competition. Consequently, no one was surprised when the National Chairman of the Democratic Party called Ed one day. The party official wanted to know if Ed had in stock a mule with an attractive mane and tail, a bit on the young side. It so happened that Ed had just acquired four such beauties at a sale up in Iowa. However, Ed had no intention of parting with any of his show mules, but he was also a reasonable man.

Hence, when the politico said, "Would you relinquish one of your fine mules for a good cause?" Ed replied that he would if the cause was a worthy one, but it would have to be very worthy. The National Chairman reminded Ed that he had been a loyal Democrat for a long time. Ed replied that he had been so loyal that he had even voted for Al Smith in 1928.

The Chairman then put the squeeze on by asking Ed to donate the mule to become the mascot for the Democratic Party. After all, Ed was a Missourian and so was President Truman. Ed repeated that he was a good Democrat, but not that good. And so a price was agreed upon, for Ed was a mule trader. And so the mule went off to Washington where he was greeted by all the high-placed Demos. There was an interesting picture in the newspapers of Senator J. Howard McGrath, Chairman of the Democratic National Committee, whispering political secrets and instructions into the mule's large ears. After many good will tours around the country, he finally ended up in Hollywood and became a celebrated movie star, Francis, the talking mule.

Although it sounded unbelievable, certain Texas Representatives said that it happened. The story involved Harry Hopkins, Franklin Roosevelt's most trusted and worthy adviser. Hopkins had grown up in Iowa, the son of a saddle and harness maker. Anyway, the following statement by Hopkins was reported in *The New York Times* in October, 1935:

"Gentlemen, we are going to increase the mule power of this country. I propose to have the farmers raise bigger and bigger mules. To do this, the government will give each farmer a mare mule so that the mule tribe may be increased. The trouble today is that there are not enough mare mules for breeding purposes on the farms."

A Texas Representative claimed he heard Hopkins make the statement and that Hopkins had his remarks removed from the Congressional Record when he discovered the facts of mule life and the evidence that he was not a genius in mule raising. Certainly, the Congressman had a wonderful time telling this story to Texas farmers.

Some critics of the New Deal, and later, the New Frontier, carried the story much further. A letter was composed to raise funds for a statue in honor of J. F. Kennedy. The letter went as follows:

"I have the distinguished honor of being a member of a Committee to raise money for a statue in honor of President Kennedy.

The Committee is in quite a quandary about a proper location for the statue. It was thought unwise to place it beside that of George Washington, who never told a lie, nor beside that of FDR who never told the truth, since John could never tell the difference.

After careful consideration, we think it should be placed beside the statue of Christopher Columbus, the greatest "New Dealer" of them all, in that he started out not knowing where he was going, and in arriving, did not know where he was, and in returning, did not know where he had been, and did it all on borrowed money.

Five thousand years ago, Moses said to the children of Israel: "Pick up your shovels, mount your asses and camels, and I will lead you to the promised land."

Nearly five thousand years later, Roosevelt said: "Lay down your shovels, sit on your asses, light up a camel. This is the promised land."

Now Kennedy is stealing the shovels, kicking your asses, raising the price of camels, and taking over the promised land."

We will expect a generous contribution from you for this worthy project."

Machiavelli had urged potential political leaders that they must play the alternate roles of both lion and fox. Stewart Alsop drew upon this lesson to comment upon the presidency of Richard Nixon. Alsop admitted that Nixon certainly knew how to be a lion and how to be a fox. He then concluded that there was yet another symbol-animal in Nixon, namely, the ass. Nixon got into the "...worst trouble of any modern President—and the basic reason is that he has done, or permitted to be done for him, some of the most asinine things in American political history." Alsop ended his column by saying that "...to an astonishing extent, Richard Nixon can also be an ass, and that is his downfall."

Drawing upon the imagery of Machiavelli, Robert Bradford, writing in the *Harvard Business Review*, said: "To live long in politics, you must possess the hide of a rhinoceros, the memory of an elephant, the persistence of a beaver, the native friendliness of a mongrel pup. You need the heart of a lion and the stomach of an ostrich. And it helps to have the humor and ubiquity of the crow. But all of these combined are not enough unless when it comes to matters of principle you also have the ornery stubbornness of the army mule."

Certainly the politicos have conspired against the jackass. He could have a bad name and image. It's a wonder he survived it all. Surely, the Democrats will keep it going. Dick Wright had a cartoon in March, 1993. Two Democratic jackasses were having a beer in what looked like "Mr. Dooley's" favorite bar. One jackass said: "I'm worried about the Republicans." The second jackass replied: "Worried? Everybody knows WE control the White House and Congress. The GOP is powerless to stop us. Don't worry, we'll get full credit for everything we do." The first jackass then mourned: "Exactly."

Chapter Five

The Mule in Court

"The law, sir, is an ass." (Charles Dickens)

At one time or another, most people would agree with Dickens. Over the years, many courts of law have had to struggle over judgments involving the mule and jackass. One can readily see that such subject matter could humble a jurist rather quickly and easily. On the other hand, mule cases, for whatever reasons, motivated the legal minds to deeper reasoning and more glowing language than normally found in legal records.

There is clear evidence in the following legal cases that the mule had a special ability to capture attention and to provoke philosophical speculation about reality and nature. What was a mule anyway? Where and how did the mule originate? Is he capable of being gentle and manageable? Why does the court refer to the mule legally as "nullius filius" (bastard or son of no one)? Whatever the opinions on these and other questions, the incidents and cases here mentioned give ample proof to the specialness and the unique feelings which the mule and jackass generated.

At one time the courthouse was geographically and socially the center of town. People came to court as a welcome excuse to postpone farm chores, to meet friends, and to "catch up" on the news. Those who could "farm out" everyday farm tasks came and stayed for the entire session, even though their cases were not on the docket. Some would actually sleep on the floor of the courtroom to be sure of a seat when the court opened for business in the morning.

The convening of the court never failed to arouse excitement. Lawyers "bristled" before the sound of the gavel like thoroughbreds waiting at the starting gate. The audience was equally eager, avidly watching the selection of the jury, listening carefully to the testimony, and trying to anticipate the verdict. The spectators didn't miss the slightest innuendo, the tiniest grimace, which might reveal innocence or guilt, defeat or victory.

Lawyers paid little attention to law books but relied on oratorical skill and psychological powers to turn a decision in their favor. Today, the golden tongued orators and "adversary" attorneys tend to resemble two businessmen negotiating rather than giant minds contending over justice and right.

Once a young lawyer argued his first case and had to contend with his own nervousness and unsureness. Moreover, he was opposed by veteran barristers representing a large railroad corporation. The case centered around the plight of a poor farmer's widow, suing for compensation for her husband's death which had occurred at a railroad crossing in the dark of the moon. The husband-farmer was driving a stubborn mule which abruptly halted in the middle of the tracks and, in typical mulish fashion, refused to budge.

The affluent railroad corporation had hired the best talent of the biggest law firm in the state. They relied on the testimony of the crossroad watchman who seemed beyond reproach. He swore before the court that he had been standing at the crossing, waving a lantern like mad. There seemed to be no doubt as to who was at fault, the mule of course. Thinking quickly, the young lawyer exposed the weakness of his opponents' argument.

"Was the lantern lit?"

"Well, no," the watchman confessed.

The number of cases which hinged upon the darkness of the night is intriguing. Abraham Lincoln once induced a witness to say clearly and in a loud voice that he had seen Lincoln's client commit a crime in bright moonlight. Lincoln challenged this testimony by displaying a farmer's almanac indicating the night passed in the dark of the moon. The almanac noted that only a fingernail rim of the moon was visible on this night, not enough to see one's nose.

Will Green, one of the old-time Ozark lawyers used to tell the history of an incident down in Greene County. Two men stole a mule and later one of them was accused of the crime. The other man, more experienced in petty crime and the tactics of prosecuting attorneys, advised the accused man on what to say when questioned.

"Where were you on said night?"

"With you."

The professional thief: "Say we were hunting."

"Was it a light or dark night?"

"I've forgotten."

"Say it was a dark night. They always make it out that way, so you might as well say it was dark as pitch."

"How could you see your watch?"

"I don't know."

"You say that we built a campfire and you saw the dial of your watch in the fire's glow."

The case came to trial and the accomplice took the witness stand.

Prosecutor: Where were you on the night of February second at ten o'clock?

Accused: I was hunting in a field outside of town.

Prosecutor: How did you know it was ten o'clock?

Accused: I pulled out my watch and looked at it.

Prosecutor: Was it a light or dark night?

Accused: Darkest night I ever see'd.

Prosecutor: How could you see your watch then?

Accused: I was waiting on my dogs to come in. So, on accounta the dogs, I built a fire. I looked at my watch in the light of the fire.

The prosecutor scratched his head in deliberation, turned away, and was about to give up the case. Suddenly he turned to the suspect: "What were you hunting?" The accused answered: "Squirrels."

The prosecutor then turned to the Judge and said: "Your honor, any man who hunts squirrels at night is either a crazy, a fool, or a liar. If the court does not find this man guilty of being crazy, foolish, or a downright liar, I am going to surrender my license."

When the two men were being led to the county jail, the second said to the first, "You never told me what we were hunting."

Another time, Champ Clark told about two of his neighbors in Pike County. These two gentlemen were prosperous farmers and good friends until they got into a heated argument over the possession of a scrub mule. So as to hurt no feelings, Clark called the farmers Jones and Brown. Each one believed that he held clear and uncontestable title to the long eared "animule."

Jones employed a widely known lawyer by the name of Broadhead, who promptly instituted suit. When the papers were served on Brown, he did not notice that Broadhead was Jones's attorney. Since Broadhead was also Brown's favorite attorney, he applied to the Colonel to represent him. Broadhead, with profound thanks for this complimentary friendship by the other side, declined.

"Well," said Brown, "I'm awfully sorry, perhaps you can recommend another lawyer for me?" "Yes, I can do that. Do you know John B. Henderson?" "No." "Well, he is the second best lawyer in the county. I will write you a letter of introduction to him."

Broadhead wrote the letter and carefully sealed it with his own coat of arms in wax. Brown left Broadhead's office and went home in a frame of mind toward the letter much resembling Mother Eve's attitude toward the forbidden fruit. The more he thought of it, the more he wanted to read it. At last he could stand it no longer. He steamed the envelope over a boiling tea kettle and pulled out the precious contents. With bulging eyes, he read:

> Dear John,
>
> Jones v. Brown. I represent the plaintiff and
> this will introduce you to the defendant. Mule
> case. Both fat.
>
> > Yours,
> > Broadhead

It was all Greek to Brown. His last condition was worse than the first. He read it right side up, bottom side up, catty-corner, diagonally, and every other way. To save his life, he couldn't understand it or get heads or tails of the mysterious and enigmatical epistle. As he tossed in sleepless anxiety, snatches of the incomprehensible message chased through his feverish brain something in this manner:

Mule case, both fat, both fat, mule case, mule fat, both case, fat case, both mule, case mule, fat both. What on earth did Broadhead mean? He says both are fat. There's only one mule and he ain't so damned fat either. Over and over it went, but finally he got it through his noggin what "both" referred to in the letter. Then he shook with laughter. He uttered a couple of objurgations: "Broadhead! Henderson! Both fat! Mule! Hades!"

Next morning, bright and early, he hied over to neighbor Jones, called him out on the porch, shook his hand warmly, showed him the letter, told him of his experience, and then delivered an opinion as full of wisdom as would befit Solomon: "Jones, you have a good farm; I have another. This measly mule isn't worth over $20. If we go to the law about it, in twelve months Jim will be living on your farm, John Henderson on mine, and we will be out in the cold. We'd be a pair of prize jackasses to do that. Let's settle the blamed case here and now between ourselves. And settle it they did, by halving the mule."

Broadhead's fat mule story obtained much notoriety in northeast Missouri. It gave birth to other stories. Once a lawyer was asked what kind of bird he would like to be if that were possible. The attorney replied: "A Vulture."

That figured.

When the mule actually did come before the court, he frequently precipitated a battle of technicalities. Everyone would agree that a mule was a mule, but beyond that, there was only agreement on disagreement. Was the mule's legal status the same as that of a horse? Could he be included in the generic heading of "livestock"?

These two questions came before the court in 1869 when Jack Cole, an Illinois farmer, lost a mule in a railway accident. Cole's mule had become unduly mulish and stood pat on a railroad track in the face of an oncoming train. Unintimidated, the locomotive ran him down.

Farmer Cole took his grievance to court. The jury heard the case and sympathized with the farmer and found the railroad company guilty of negligence. Cole was awarded compensation for his deceased mule under an 1855 law which provided that railroad companies must make and maintain fences sufficient to prevent "cattle and horses" from getting on the roadbed.

The Railroad appealed the decision to a higher court. Here the attorney contended that his company had fully complied with the law, and, furthermore, Cole's suit had no relevancy since the mule was neither a cow nor a horse. In due time, the Cole mule case worked its way through the Illinois courts until it reached the State Supreme Court. Learned and distinguished justices then deliberated on the character of the mule. Eventually, the Court rejected the railroad company's argument and upheld the case of Jack Cole and his dead mule. The justices based their opinion upon an earlier decision of the same court which held that a jackass was legally and rightfully included within the meaning of a statute which merely specified "horses and cattle." Thus the Supreme Court justices held: "It is not going too far in this case to say that a mule comes nearer to a horse than an ass...."

Even when the mule was accepted as "just a plain old mule," the courts were confronted with more complex questions. "Were all mules

53

similarly situated? Were there good mules and bad mules? Gentle mules and not-so-gentle mules? Or, were all mules inherently dangerous and incapable of domesticity?" In struggling with these questions, the courts weighed the "doctrine of contributory negligence" and the principle of the "last clear chance."

The latter principle was asserted in a famous jackass case. A willful donkey strayed on the highway and was injured by a careless driver. The judge declared that even though the ass was negligent, the driver, with ordinary care, had the "last clear chance" to avoid the accident and had failed to do so. Hence, while the mule's papa, the jackass, was admittedly in the wrong, the court recognized greater negligence on the part of the careless driver.

In later cases, however, the mule was not granted this reasoning. In fact, in 1900, a Kansas City court averred that all mules everywhere were so inherently dangerous as to constitute a distinct threat to the general welfare.

The case arose out of an accident on a street improvement project in Kansas City. The foreman of the Falk Construction Company ordered an employee, Pete Borden, to connect the tongue of a bending machine to a wagon which was pulled by two mules. The foreman promised to control the mules while Pete Borden went under the wagon to do the job. Borden followed instructions, climbed underneath, and attempted to hook the tongue of the bending machine to the wagon. While "hunkered" on his left knee, the mules became unruly, jerked the wagon and pulled the 6,000 pound bending machine over Borden's foot and severely injured it. Meanwhile the foreman was standing in front of the team but not supervising them adequately.

Pete Borden sued for the recovery of damages in the Circuit Court of Kansas City and was awarded a judgment against the Falk Construction Company. The company appealed to the Kansas City Court of Appeals. Shortly, this Court handed down what proved to be the "Dred Scott" decision in mule litigation.

In rejecting the company's brief, the Court upheld Pete Borden's claim for recovery and rebuked the foreman for failure to take a firm grip on the mules. But that was not all. The opinion contained one of the most blatant *obiter dictum* rulings ever written. Justice Smith, in his remarks, offered a few gratuitous comments about the mule. "The mule is a domestic animal whose treacherous and vicious nature is so well known that the courts may take judicial notice of it. The owner of such an animal cannot be heard to say that he did not know of its treacherous and unreliable character."

Such an arbitrary pronouncement could not be permitted to pass unnoticed. Newspapers throughout the State of Missouri rose in righteous indignation and protested the stereotyping of Missouri's most famous product. One metropolitan paper labelled the sweeping sentence as "...obviously unfair and decidedly unwarranted. The long-eared and long legged animal, the Missouri Mule, deserves the right of appeal to the Supreme Court of Missouri."

The mule finally did get a hearing before Missouri's highest tribunal, but the appeal did not come on the Borden case. Fifteen years elapsed before the mule had his day. In the interval, several other court cases in other states stigmatized the mule. In 1907, James Walker sued the Manufacturers Fuel Company in the Illinois courts for financial restitution due to an injury sustained while working one of the company's mules.

Pete, the company mule, was strong, high spirited, and had a relatively good service record. Prior to the accident, Pete was accustomed to pulling one car of coal at a time on a clean track. This was considered a normal assignment. On the eventful day of the accident, Pete was ordered to pull two cars over a track littered with slate and cinders. Pete figured "enough was enough" and showed his displeasure by kicking vigorously. James White, a fellow employee, got in the way of Pete's lethal hoofs and had to be hospitalized. White took his case against the company and the mule to court and recovered $1750 in compensation for the loss of his right kidney.

Then a Kentucky decision threatened to push the public's attitude toward the mule to a new low. The incident leading to the court case occurred on a ferry boat. As was the practice at the time, a seventy-five foot craft was propelled by an old gray mare walking endlessly on an inclined treadway which was connected to a paddle wheel which powered the boat across the river.

On the morning of November 6, 1905, L. R. Terrell drove his mule team and wagon onto S. W. Tolin's ferry. To protect his mules, in the event of an accident to the boat on the river crossing, Terrell began unhitching his team. In the midst of the operation, the mare horse powering Tobin's ferry reached over the framework and bit one of Terrell's mules on the rump. At precisely the same moment, Terrell unwisely chose to go behind his mule team to pick up the lines. Reacting either to the mare's bite or to Terrell's strategic location behind his heels, one of the mules did the natural thing. He kicked.

When the smoke cleared, Terrell was in the hospital suffering permanent injury. The lower court granted Terrell $5,000 recovery for damages, but the Appeals Court disavowed the claim. The State Supreme Court followed the decision of the Appeals Court in placing the responsibility at the foot of the mule. Said the court:

(1) It is a matter of common knowledge that the mule is prone to kick and there is no way of telling when or under what circumstances a mule will or will not kick.

(2) The only way to escape danger from the feet of a mule is not to go within the radius of his heels.

(3) He who goes within these limits assumes the risk of being kicked, especially when (he does so) without warning to the mule…."

Thus the mule was acknowledged to be inherently depraved and not incidentally capricious or whimsical. The consequences of such reasoning were immediately apparent. An employer need no longer exercise care in the selection and supervision of the mules which he provided for his employees. He would not have to inquire into the disposition and temperament of his mules, but he could conclude, as apparently the court had done, that all mules are dangerous. Therefore, anyone taking a job working with mules should know beforehand what to expect. He had no claim for redress in the event the mule reacted unfavorably to his presence.

Fortunately a series of court decisions in other states mitigated the result of the Kentucky decision and restored the mule's self-respect. In 1911, a North Carolina court ruled that a team of mules and a wagon were not inherently a dangerous instrumentality. In the same year, the St. Louis Court of Appeals ruled that there was such a thing as a gentle mule, even a gentle Missouri mule.

After being kicked by a company mule while hanging up the mule's harness, August Stutske suffered complications that ultimately resulted in the amputation of his leg. In the litigation that followed, the company argued that mules as a class are dangerous and apt to kick. The mule's traits were so apparent, the company contended that a man of ordinary prudence would take all necessary precautions while working around them. The Court was unimpressed. A more accurate view, the Court argued, would be to acknowledge the existence of gentle mules, mules not addicted to kicking, and thus non-dangerous mules.

Two minor classics from the legal literature are "The Celebrated Jackass Case" in Nebraska and "The Celebrated Mule Case" in Missouri. First, the Jackass Case and the opinion of Justice Oliver of the Nebraska Court of Appeals:

"The evidence before the Court is amply sufficient to establish an express warranty on the part of the defendant that the animal in question was a fit and suitable one for breeding purposes, and the Court therefore finds that there was a warranty. But even conceding that there was no warranty, there surely can be no question, under the evidence, that there was an implied warranty as to its fitness as a breeder and foal-getter. The defendant must surely have known that the plaintiff was purshasing the animal for breeding purposes only. He knew at the time of making the sale that no reasonable man would attempt to use a jackass for any other purpose than to outrage nature by propagating mules. He could not have supposed that the plaintiff desired to acquire a jackass for a pet. The animal is wholly unsuitable for that purpose. Its form is neither pleasing to the eye, nor its voice soothing to the ear. He is neither ornamental in his appearance, nor amusing in his habits; he is valuable only as he is able and willing to propagate the mule species.

"It appears from the evidence that after purchasing the animal, the plaintiff on several occasions caused him to be placed in the society of certain soft-eyed, sleek-coated young mares, that were in the pink of that condition which is supposed to arouse the interest and attract the attention of any reasonably amorous jackass, but that he passed them up and knew them not. The defendant admits representing to the plaintiff that the jackass in question would do that work for himself. But evidence shows that if he was ever possessed of that valuable and charming accomplishment, he failed on the occasions just mentioned to practice it with the zeal and ardor becoming of an ambitious jackass in full possession of his faculties.

"He was, indeed, a worthless, unpedigreed and impotent jackass, without pride of ancestry or hope of posterity—a source of disappointment to his female friends, and an item of expense to his owner. There is no brute in all the animal kingdom more worthless than a Missouri-bred jackass afflicted with lost manhood. He was not as represented and warranted by the defendant, and the plaintiff is entitled to recover." (121 Neb.App. 72).

Not to be outdone by Nebraska, Missouri had its own "Celebrated Mule Case". Surprisingly this controversy, Lyman v. Dale, involved a mere sum of five dollars. Yet the arguments were heard before four different courts, stretched out for a period of more than five years, involved three different opinions in the Court of Appeals, and two opinions in the Missouri Supreme Court. The case cost the State of Missouri approximately $5,000 before it was adjudicated. The concurring opinion which terminated the case was one of the best written, certainly the most humorous, in the annals of Missouri jurisprudence.

The events attending the case were simple enough: B. L. Lyman and his two companions were driving a horse and buggy along a relatively quiet street in Springfield, Missouri. The street was under repair and, at one point, there was an open pit banked by a rick of bricks and dirt. A red light had been placed upon the embankment as a warning to all wayfarers. As Lyman and his two companions approached the hazard in the road, they were met by a Mr. Parker, riding one mule and leading another. The mules belonged to Horace Dale, a neighboring farmer, who employed Parker to work his animals.

As the buggy and mule approached each other from opposite directions, the mule Parker was leading became skittish and pulled over toward Lyman's buggy. The rear end of the mule and the front end of the buggy made contact. Instinctively the mule whipped his right hind leg in between the shaft and the wheel, poked out numerous spokes, and thoroughly upset the occupants.

The dispute over liability and damages began undramatically in the office of the Justice of the Peace in Springfield. At the hearing, Lyman was awarded a recovery of five dollars, the cost of replacing the wheel. Dale, however, refused to accept the ruling that his mules were responsible. He appealed to the Circuit Court. In a new trial in Circuit Court, Lyman was again favored and awarded the $5 in damages.

Dale was a stubborn Missourian. He refused to admit defeat and carried the case to the Circuit Court of Appeals. Here the five dollar mule case evoked a majority opinion, a separate concurring opinion, and a dissenting opinion. In a majority opinion of six pages, upholding Lyman's petition, Judge Argus Cox wrote: "…that there should be some limit to the amount of rope given to a Missouri mule in a public street of a city is self-evident. It is also clear that a man leading a high spirited mule…should use greater precaution and hold the mule closer to himself…."

In a concurring opinion, Judge J. P. Nixon cited the mule as contributory cause of negligence. Nevertheless, the mule case refused to die. A third judge, Howard Gray, sparked new hope for Dale in a ten page dissenting opinion. Judge Gray noted that Dale's mules were gentle and well-broken. Both parties had agreed to this fact.

Lyman himself had testified: "I did not notice anything alarming about those mules. Nothing more than common." His brother had said: "The mule seemed to be coming along very nicely." Parker insisted: "They were a little high-lifted mules, but they were well broke for young mules."

Judge Gray continued: "My brethren say: 'There should be some limit to the amount of rope given a Missouri mule in a public street is self-evident.' With this statement, I fully agree without limiting its application to a Missouri mule."

The point of Judge Gray's dissent was that the halter was of ordinary length and the mules were not wild nor unruly. If Dale was held in liability, then every farmer in the state would have to cease the long accustomed practice of leading horses and mules with a halter of ordinary length when traveling on the highways and public streets. In summary, Judge Gray suggested an appeal to the Supreme Court.

Three and a half years later, the case did appear on the docket of the highest court in Missouri. Two lawyers, W. D. Hubbard and J. T. White represented Dale. They argued that leading a mule, particularly a Missouri mule, by the halter was the only sensible way, that leading a mule with a five-foot halter was not negligent, since that is as close as one would care to come to a Missouri mule, and that the street obstruction, and not the Missouri mule, was the cause of the accident.

The plaintiff, Lyman, filed no brief, but rested his case solely upon the decisions of the lower court, which, of course, were in his favor. Lyman apparently felt all had been said that could be said.

State Supreme Court Justice Waller W. Green wrote the findings of the Court. He began: "A yellow slip of paper found in the files bears the ominous inscription, THE CELEBRATED MULE CASE, and nothing more. Why we were thus enlightened by this otherwise silent monitor, we know not. It, at least, admonishes us to look well to the facts."

The judge did look well at the facts. After thoroughly reviewing the evidence, the Court reversed the previous decision holding that any other judgment would overturn all common knowledge of handling animals on the common highways.

"We regret to feel constrained to thus abruptly terminate THE CELEBRATED MULE CASE, but it should have been so determined long since. Let the judgment of the Circuit Court be simply reversed so there will be an end to the controversy."

The famous mule case was not quite finished. While all the justices were in complete agreement that Dale and his mule should be vindicated, the last word had not been realized. The Chief Justice, Henry Lamm, offered a concurring opinion. Besides being a literary document, Lamm's commentary was the most substantially clever opinion ever handed down by a Missouri jurist.

The Chief Justice wrote: "...Beginning with the J.P.'s, it (The mule case) has reached the P.J.'s, and its journey has run the gamut of three courts, one above the other. Now, it, a fuss over five dollars, has reached the highest court in the state for final disposition. However, if the amount is small, the value of the case for doctrine's sake is great.

"As I see it, the case is this: Dale, a man of substance, a farmer, owned a brown and a gray mule, both young and of fine growth; one saddle-wise, the other, otherwise. Both, used to the plow and wagon, were entitled to the designation 'well-broken and gentle.' One Parker was Dale's manservant and, in the usual course of his employment, had charge of these mules.

"On a certain day he had driven them to a water wagon in the humble office of supplying water to a clover huller in the Ozark region hard by the metropolis, towit, Springfield. Eventide had fallen, i.e., the poetical time of day had come when the beetle wheels his droning flight, drowsy tinkling lulls the distant folds and all the air a solemn stillness holds. In other words, dropping into the vernacular, it was time to 'take-out.'

"Accordingly, Parker took out, with his mind fixed on the watch dog's honest bark baying deep-mouthed welcome as he drew near home. He mounted the rideable mule. He says he tied the other to the hames of the harness on the ridden one by a four or five foot halter rope, and was plodding his weary way homeward a la the plowman in the Elegy.

"The viccissitudes of the journey in due course brought him to Walnut Street in said city of Springfield. At a certain place in that street, the city fathers had broken the pavement and made a 'rick of bricks' aside a long hole or ditch. Hard by this 'rick of bricks' was a ridge of fresh earth capped by a display of red-lantern danger signals.

It seems the unridden mule crowded against the ridden one and harassed Parker by coming in scraping contact with his circumjacent leg. Any boy who ever rode the lead horse in harrowing his father's field will get the idea.

"In this pickle, he took hold of the halter rope, still fastened to the hames, to keep the unridden mule from rasping his said leg. As will be seen later on, at this point, a grave question arises, towit, is it negligence to lead a mule by hand or should he be fastened 'neck and neck' to his fellows? But we anticipate.

"Going back a little, it seems as follows: At about the time Parker had reached said part of Walnut Street, plaintiff and two others were in a buggy pulled by a single horse and on their way home to the country. So equipped these several parties met face to face. At this point it will do to say that while the mules were used to being on the water wagon, it is not so clear that these travelers three were. There are signs of that artificial elation in the vehicle party that in the evening springs from drinking (breathing freely) but in the morning after produces the condition of voluntary expiation that Dr. Von Ihring calls 'katzenjammer'. They disavow being half-seas over or drunk;.

"Their chief spokesman, as descriptive of the situation, in part told his story mathematically in this fashion: 'I had not drunk so much but what I kept count. I can keep count until I take three and HADN'T QUIT COUNTING YET.' In the course of their journey, they, too, came to the brick rick, the ditch, the ridge of dirt, and the red lights on Walnut Street. There they met, as said, the gray and brown mule and Parker face to face. When the mules and rider approached and passed the three travelers, all on the same side of the ditch, the lead mule, whether scared by the hole in the ground, the rick of bricks, or the ridge, is dark, shied from his fellow ('spread himself') and presently his hind leg was mixed up with the shafts and wheel of the buggy. When the *status quo ante* was reestablished, both leg and wheel were found to be damaged. Subsequently a blacksmith offered to repair the damage to the wheel for, say, a dollar and a half. This sum, the defendant, though denying liability, was willing and offered to pay; but the plaintiff's dander was up and he, as buggy owner, demanded a new wheel worth five dollars, and sued.

"In the Justice Court, defendant lost outright and appealed. In the Circuit Court, the same. The learned judges of the Court of Appeals could not agree (the *furor scribendi* being much in evidence and three learned opinions falling from their several pens) and sent the case here, and here it is.

"My brother Graves has well disposed of it on certain grounds, but the theme being the Missouri mule and state pride calling for further exposition, the said *furor scribendi* has seized me—witness:

"a) It is argued that it was negligence to ride one mule and lead its fellow by hand. That they should be halter-yoked 'neck and neck'. Parker says he necked them in a way, but plaintiff takes issue on the fact. Allowing credit to plaintiff's evidence, two questions spring, *viz.*: First, is the neck and neck theory 'mule law' in this jurisdiction? Second, if so, then was the absence of the neck and neck adjustment the proximate cause of the injury?

"We may let the first question be settled in some other mule case and pass to the second as more important. It will be observed that the neck and forequarters of the mule did not do the damage. Contra, the hind quarters, or 'business end' of the mule were in fault. We take judicial notice of the facts of nature. Hence, we know that haltering a mule neck and neck to another will not prevent his hind parts spreading. His neck might be on one line, but his hind legs and heels might be on another, a divergent one. True, the mental concept relating to shying or spreading would naturally originate in the mule's head.

"But it must be allowed as a sound psychological proposition that haltering his head or neck can in nowise control the mule's thoughts or control the hinder parts affected by those thoughts. So much, I think, is clear and is due to be said of the Missouri mule, whose bones, in attestation of his activity and worth, lie bleaching from Shiloh to Spion Kop, from San Juan to Przemyal (pronounced, I am told by a scholar, as it is spelled).

"It results that causal connection between the negligence in hand and the injury is broken and recovery cannot go on the neck-and-neck theory. This because it is plain under the distances disclosed by the evidence that the mule's hind legs could reach the buggy wheel in spite of a neck-and-neck attachment.

"(b) The next question is a bit elusive, but seems lodged in the case. It runs thus: There being no evidence to show the mule was 'wild and unruly' as charged, is such a mule per se a nuisance, a vicious animal, has he a heart devoid of social duty and fatally bent on mischief when led by a halter on the street of a town, and must his owner answer for his acts on that theory?

"Attend to that view of it:

(l) There are sporadic instances of mules behaving badly. That one that Absolom rode and 'went from under' him at a crisis in his fate, for instance. So it had been intimated in fireside precepts that the mule is UNEXPECTED in his heel action, and has other faults. In Spanish folk lore it is said: He who wants a mule without fault must walk. So, at the French chimney-corner the adage runs: The mule long keeps a kick in reserve for his master. The mule don't kick according to no rule, said the American Negro. His (the mule) voice has been a matter of derision and there be those who put their tongue in their cheek when speaking of it. Witness the German proverb: Mules make a great fuss about their ancestors having been asses. And so on. But none of these things are factors in the instant case; for here there was no kicking and no braying standing in relation of *causa causans* to the injury to the wheel.

"Moreover, the rule of logic is that induction which proceeds by merely citing instances is childish affair and...it may be overthrown by contrary instances. Accordingly, the faithfulness, the dependableness, the surefootedness, the endurance, the strength, and the good sense of the mule, all matters of common knowledge, may be allowed to stand over against his faults and create either an equilibrium or a preponderance in the scales in his favor. He, then, as a domestic animal is entitled to the doctrine that if he becomes vicious, guilty knowledge (the *scienter*) must be brought home to his master, precisely as it must be on the dog or ox. The rule of the master's liability of the ox is old. That for the acts of the dog is put this way: the law allows the dog the first bite....So with the mule.

"Absent proof of the bad habit of 'spreading' when led and the scienter, liability did not spring from the mere fact that his hind leg (he being scared) got over the wheel while he was led by a five-foot halter rope; for it must be held that a led mule is not a nuisance per se, unless he is to be condemned on that score out-and-out because of his ancestry, and some law of heredity, some asinine rule, so to speak, a question which we take next.

"(2) Some care should be taken not to allow such scornful remarks as that 'the mule has no pride of ancestry or hope of posterity' to press upon our judgment. He inherits his father's ears, but what of that? The ass's ears, presented by an angry Apollo, were an affliction to King Midas, but not to the mule. He is a hybrid, but that was man's invention centuries gone in some province in Asia Minor, and the fact is not chargeable to the mule. So the slowness of the domestic ass does not descend as a trait to the Missouri mule. It is said that thistle is fat

63

salad for an ass's mouth. Maybe it is also in a mule's, but be it so, surely his penchant for homely fare cannot so far condemn him that he does not stand *rectus in curia*. Moreover, if his sire stands in satire as an emblem of sleepy stupidity, yet that avails naught; for the authorities…agree that the Missouri mule takes after his dam and not his sire in that regard. All asses are not four-footed, the adage saith, and yet to call a man an 'ass' is quite a different thing than to call him 'mulish' (vide, the lexicographers).

"Furthermore, the very word jackass is a term of reproach everywhere, as in the literature of law. Do we not all know that a certain phase of the law of negligence, the humanitarian rule, first announced, it has been said, in a donkey case (Davies v. Mann, 10 Mees. & Wels. 545) has been called, by those who deride it, the 'jack-ass doctrine?' This on the doctrine of the adage: call a dog by a bad name and then hang him. But, on the other hand, to sum up fairly, it was an ass that saw the heavenly vision, even Balaam, the seer, could not see and first raised a voice against cruelty to animals. (Num. 22:23 et seq.) So, did not Sancho Panza by meditation gather sparks of wisdom while ambling along on the back of one, that radiated in his wonderful judgments pronounced in his decision by the common-sense rule of knotty cases in the Island of Barataria? Did not Samson use the jawbone of one effectually on a thousand Philistines? Is not his name imperishably preserved in that of the fifth proposition of the first book of Euclid—the *pons asinorum*?

"But we shall pursue the subject no farther. Enough has been said to show that the ass is not without some rights in the courts even on sentimental grounds; ergo, if his hybrid son, tracing his lineage as he does to the Jacks of Kentucky and Andalusia, inherits some of his traits cannot be held bad *per se, Q.E.D.*

"It is meet that a five-dollar case, having its tap root in anger (and possibly in liquor), should drag its slow lengths through the courts for more than five years, even if it had earned the sobriquet of 'celebrated mule case.'"

After such judicial perspicacity, it might be fitting to close this judiciary chapter with the ficticious lawsuit brought by a retired Superior Court judge, William G. Long, in the World Court of Public Conscience. Long was offended deeply that the animal (jack-ass) was so often ridiculed and villified because of things that were not of its doing. Judge Long wanted the animal to be more appreciated and recognized for its long and faithful service throughout history.

In the course of his argument before the world jury, Long made a very important distinction between "jackass and jack-ass." Long asked the public to use jackass to refer to the human jackasses, and jack-ass to the animal jackasses. (The reader could do it the opposite way as long as the reader was consistent.) If *homo sapiens* would keep this dividing line in mind, much of the low regard, ridicule, malediction, and abuse would be more accurately directed at the jackass, while the jack-ass would receive the honor and adulation due it. In this manner, justice would be advanced to a higher level and civilization greatly enhanced.

———— Chapter Six ————

Mule Trading

"It's possible for a mule trader to be honest. But it isn't very probable." Missouri Folklore.

The arrival of the mule trader and his mules provided great excitement in many Missouri towns. There were shouts, sundry expletives, imprecations not found in the Book of Prayer, and the musical tattoo of leather and rawhide whips on the backside of the mules. The commotion often exceeded that caused by the Wells Fargo delivery wagon. Anxious mothers scurried about warning and collecting their small children out of harm's way.

The refractory mules were simply interesting in their own unpredictable manner. When they behaved decently and moved quietly to the persuasive eloquence of the prod, it was generally understood that their apparent good manners were either an accident or an expedient. For in the next moment, the intractable animals were back in character again, dashing for an open yard gate. Once inside a villager's front yard, the mules would roll in the flower beds, dance around the rambler roses, taste the leaves of hollyhock and lilac, until, in unrestrained anger, the traders would drive them back to the road.

Coming from afar, stopping only for a day, sometimes advertised in advance, the mule trader captured the imagination of many a Missouri child. The trader had the air of the unfamiliar, the suggestive allure of the outside world. The mule trader was a merchant adventurer. Shrewdness was his stock-in-trade and he had to be knowledgeable about many things.

Engaged in one of the most competitive of all activities, the mule trader became a paragon of virtues and vices. He had to be as canny as a tight-lipped Yankee pedlar, be able to outtalk a pitchman at a county fair or a politician for that matter, be able to drive a rough and ready bargain on the village square, and then turn around to wine and dine some sophisticated wealthy farmer or southern planter.

When times were good, the trader smoked thirty-five cent Mercantile cigars and drank Kentucky rye in eight-sided bottles which was so "smoothe" you could drink enough of it to become intoxicated. When times were slack and trades were few and far between, dining on roast beef and Bordeaux wine changed quickly to a menu of canned tomatoes and crackers.

Regardless of economic circumstances, the same recognizable symbols commanded a trader's rank and station, the wide-brimmed stetson, red-figured neckerchief, jeweled stick-pin, stockman's boots, highly carved hickory cane and a braided whip. Oh yes, there was always the inevitable diamond ring which stood out like the light on a riverboat coming upstream on a pitch black night. The ring gave the appearance of affluence and financial security, and also served well in the last round of desperate poker, or provided needed collateral for the purchase of a carload of fat mules.

The mule itself, freakish, unusual, nature's unwanted child, undoubtedly influenced the style of life and the personality of the mule trader. It may have been the mysterious and often impenetrable mind of the mule that caused the men engaged in the mule trade to be assigned intuitive wisdom, unlimited courage, and a combination of traits not commonly associated with the human family. It may have been an "Act of God" which set the mule apart from the rest of the animal kingdom coupled with the famed quadruped's "peculiar" characteristics that created in the public mind a whole cluster of expectations and beliefs about mules and the men who dealt with them.

In any event, the concept of the mule trader became typed with a touch of the dramatic and the deranged, a bit of the odd and the singular, and an overendowment of daring. In living up to an assigned role and subtly exploiting it, the mule trader was frequently a showman who realized that advertising was good sales promotion. All of the big mule traders were colorful personalities. Diamond Billy Hall of Lancaster, Missouri, mingled the roles of ringmaster and trademaster. He wore a stove-piped hat and cutaway coat even when he was knee deep in mud in the stockyard.

A wandering road trader from Callaway County, Bill Haney, bargained for mules, it was said, in every county in the United States. Bill advertised his appearance in a town with a circular stating that he would buy any mule from "Four to Forty-four."

Joe Kendig, the Pennsylvania Dutch trader from York, came to St.

Louis often and purchased as many as five carloads of mules at a time. Sometimes Kendig bought mules whether he needed them or not. "You can't keep shop without fresh stock," he would counsel his sons learning the trade. There was also the unparalleled Ferd Owens of Belton, Missouri, the last of the great mule traders, who outmanuevered the keenest traders of two continents. In the heyday of his business empire, he bought and sold 100,000 mules and horses a year. There was also Bill McVean and Ray Lum and many, many more. Each had a distinctive flair and aura.

Many of the Missouri traders came from the Kingdom of Callaway (a county in Missouri which, according to legend, never surrendered in the Civil War). Here was a tradition of trading. The land was something less than Iowa or Illinois soil. Not being able to raise bumper crops of corn or wheat, the farmers turned to raising mules and other livestock. In the passage of time, the Callaway trader emerged, willing to trade or swap anything with anybody: coon dogs, hunting knives, saddle horses or a plug mule.

At every Missouri sale, you could see the men from Callaway sitting on empty nail kegs with their backs against the side of a barn and whittling away. They always carried a soft piece of cedar wood and a knife with a blade so sharp you could see it gleaming a quarter of a mile away. The character type was unforgettable. Dave Baer of Belleville, Illinois, claimed he could spot a man from Callaway as easily as he could recognize a giraffe.

Mule traders as a group felt superior to the general run of traders, particularly horse traders. In their opinion, any one could sell horses, but it took real skill to judge a mule, purchase him, and then resell the irascible critter for more than he was worth. There was something virus-like about dealing with the cursed creatures that got into the trader's blood. Call it affection or addiction, the bond between trader and traded often went beyond the profit motive. Most often, it was the act of trading that hooked the trader. Even though they sometimes loved the animal(s), they taught themselves to love "the trade" more. This is where their livelihood existed.

Ferd Owens, Homer Leach, and the Sparks Brothers kept on selling mules after the market ceased to be profitable. Ferd Owens stayed with mules at a time when the cattle market was booming and all he would have had to do would have been to change the sign in front of his office in the Kansas City Stockyard to triple his income. Ed Frazier raised some of the finest mules in the annals of Missouri and stayed with them to his dying day. Eventually Dave Baer became a director of the First National Bank at Belleville, Illinois, yet he still maintained a separate listing in the telephone directory as a mule broker. Each spring, farmers would come to Dave and ask him to go with them to the country and examine a span of mules to see what they were worth. And Dave would always go.

Any discussion of mule trading inevitably began or ended with a commentary on the integrity of the trader. Was he an honest man? Were his activities based upon a sliding scale of ethics? Did he tell the truth? On all these questions, opinion is divided, but the greater amount of testimony supports the common conviction that "a mule trader will never tell you a lie if you understand him," or, "mule traders will tell you the truth if you speak their language."

Ray Lum would say that some people are asleep when you talk to them and he would let them sleep on. Of course his speech was so rapid-fire, that it was difficult to catch everything he was saying. And the trader had some special lingo with which a buyer had to be familiar. "Hittin" on three" meant the mule was lame in one leg. "One lamp only" told you the mule was blind in one eye. Once a trader was trying to sell a team of mules and when asked their age, the trader answered: "eleven and eleven." Did he mean the mules were twenty-two? Or each mule was eleven?

Since many farmers thought the ideal age of a mule was seven, should one be surprised to find that most mules were seven years old? Traders could tell you something forty different ways faster than you could imagine. He wouldn't lie to you as much as confuse or distract you. Often there would be a story thrown in somewhere. One trader cautioned his prospective buyer by asking the buyer not to add anything to the story when he passed it along because the trader had already added enough.

The trader loved the weaseling words or phrases which allowed them to never say exactly what the truth was. One trader said that your morals should be as loose as a politician's vest. The public wasn't surprised by the fact that many mule traders became used car dealers or politicians after the passing of the mule era. To be a successful trader, a person had to be able to sell himself and get people to trust and like them. They also had to have great facility in talking, even talking out of both sides of their mouth.

Certainly the popular image of the mule trader was a man who lied with every breath and breathed very rapidly. Ovid Bell owned and published the *Fulton Chronicle* for several decades. As a country editor, Bell probably talked to more mule traders than any man in Missouri. From his experience, he concluded: "Mule traders as a group were unhesitatingly and instinctively dishonest. They lie to you, lie without batting any eyelash. The only honest mule trader I ever met was a Presbyterian preacher over near Auxvasse and he had to be honest."

As a journalist, Bell was constantly inquiring into the status of Callaway's largest cash crop—mules. When he attempted to secure information about the market, future trends and prices, he rarely could get the truth. Bell would approach an individual widely known for the quality and the quantity of his mule crop and say: "Now I don't expect you to tell me the truth, but I would like to hear what you have to say, anyhow. How many mules are you raising this year?" Invariably the answer would be evasive. The farmer would often claim that he had gone out of the mule business, when, at the same time he was speaking, twenty to fifty mules would be in his pasture.

"Actually," continued Ovid Bell, "from my experience I doubt there ever has been an honest mule statistic to come out of the state of Missouri. You just can't get those hard-bitten farmers to tell the truth about their mules. Further, they would consistently tell you that they got twenty-five per cent more on their sales than they really received. If anything the mule traders were worse. One well known St. Louis trader came to Fulton and bought two carloads of mules. I heard about it and stopped him on a side-street and asked: 'What did you pay for mules today?'"

The trader replied: "Hell, man, I didn't even try to buy a colt. Market's too high." At the same time, Bell knew exactly how many the trader had bought and at what price.

Throughout history, traders have refused to divulge particulars about their business. So why would mule traders be an exception? A Missouri farmer once asked the fabulous road trader, Bill Haney, how he came out after a winter of heavy trading. Bill replied that he had broken the world record. The farmer explored the answer, "What do you mean by that?" Bill laughed and replied: "I broke even."

Naturally mule traders resented aspersions cast upon their honesty and integrity. They regarded themselves as fair and honorable as any other segment of the business community, or the general public for that matter. They would quote Shakespeare and say: "As honest as this world goes."

Of course there was often a fine line between deliberate fraud and honest deception. An employee of the Internal Revenue Service once visited a mule trader by the name of Sam Yalson. While supper was being prepared, Sam suddenly announced that he would have to go out to the barn and feed one of his mules. Fifteen minutes later he returned with his clothes torn, his face severely bruised and a cut on his arm. His wife made only one remark: "Sam, you simply must get rid of that mule."

A couple of months later, the agent asked Sam what happened to that troublesome mule. Sam said that he had bargained him off for a cow. "Did you tell the man about the mule's nasty disposition?" "No," answered Sam, "I cleaned forgot." Sam admitted that he thought about it later, but rationalized that the farmer was bound to find it out soon enough. He had always been taught that when two evils are present, take the lesser of the two. And so he didn't tell the farmer.

Going beyond the matter of telling the truth, the buyer had to inspect the animal carefully to make sure that the product was not being misrepresented. Old mules that had turned white or gray, could be artfully colored black. Hoofs could be painted and doctored to conceal abnormalities. Caved in pockets on the head or on the body could be inflated with air. One trader concealed the fact that a whole ear was missing by putting a hat on the mule to which was attached an artificial ear. Another mule had an artificial tail. There seemed to be no end to the tricks of the trade.

"If you are not satisfied, bring him back." So assured, the farmer bought the mule and took him home, only to find the fractious beast impossible to control. He took the mule back to the trader and expected to get his money back. But the trader reminded him that he had only been told to bring him back. Nothing was said about getting his money back.

Another time, a trader warned a farmer to look the mule right in the eye and he would never have any trouble with him. So the farmer bought him and took him home. After looking him in the eye very seriously, the farmer proceeded to hitch him up to a wagon, whereupon he got kicked like he had never been kicked before. When he took the mule back to the trader, he was told that he got kicked because he had stopped looking the mule in the eye.

It was always more interesting when the story turned against the trader. One time Dave Sparks, a St. Louis trader, was travelling north of Kansas City and saw a handsome mule in a pasture. He stopped at the house to inquire if the mule was for sale. The farmer said he was interested but the mule was a pet of the family, especially the wife. This fact also meant that the farmer was looking for the top dollar for his mule. When Sparks offered considerably less than top dollar, the farmer said that he would have to discuss the matter with his wife.

The farmer went around the house to the back porch which was screened in. A few moments later, Dave heard the most bitter family argument he had ever listened to. The wife upbraided her husband for even thinking of selling the mule. "Dan, how could you even think of selling Annie? She's a family pet. You're the kind of man who would sell his grandmother's coffin while she was still in it. If you sell Annie, you had better find yourself another bed and another house."

At that point, a stair-step array of children appeared around the corner of the house. Seeing the children, the wife began to scream: "Daddy's goin' to sell Annie." The children picked up the chorus: "Daddy's goin' to sell Annie."

Dave Sparks said to himself: "If I'm going to get Annie, I had better start buying her." By this time, the farmer had walked away from his family which was still crying and screaming. Sparks told the farmer that, under the circumstances, he would pay $125. While the children were still crying, Sparks led Annie away.

Sparks and the mule were hardly out of sight of the farm-house when Annie began to pant loudly. Her flanks were quivering and her nostrils flared out. Sparks couldn't believe what he saw and heard. Annie was windy. Sparks had been had. Annie was oversold even at $5. He wanted to turn around and go back to undo the deal. But he knew he couldn't go back on a bargain and violate a life-time policy.

As he traveled further, suspicions began to creep into his mind. He began to wonder if he had really bought a pet. Eventually he met a neighboring farmer who admitted to Dave that the entire episode, from the children up, was nothing but a well rehearsed act. Sparks couldn't believe that he had been taken in this manner. The farmer tried to console him: "You're not the first to bite into a rotten apple."

Another time, a road trader was up in Nebraska looking for mules to buy. One farm had five rather good looking mules in a pasture close by the road. The trader stopped to inquire about buying them. It turned out the farm was owned and operated by a widow with ten children. Indeed, the mules were for sale and they were exceptionally good animals. And she needed the money. She asked for the top dollar and the trader agreed because of the situation. When he loaded them up, he found every one of the animals to have a serious deficiency and worth almost nothing. The "widow" was clearly smiling as he drove off with his prizes.

On another occasion, there was a German immigrant living in central Missouri by the name of Hans Jesen. Hans was an educated man. It was alleged that he had a doctorate from a famous European University and that he could speak seven languages, all of them better than he could speak English. His neighbors observed that Hans often used his inadequacy with the English language to his own advantage. Whenever he was at a loss for a word, he hesitated, and permitted a bystander to supply it. Curiously, the word was usually the precise word Hans needed to win an argument, close a business deal, or turn a good story.

Now Hans did not raise many mules, but like all other farmers, he always had a mule or two around the place. Once a trader from Versailles, Missouri, came through looking for mules to buy. Hans was sitting in his rocker when the trader came along. "Hans, do you have any mules for sale?"

"Nein," said Hans, "I hoft von out der in der fer pasture, but he hain't ver sale. He's a vine mule, too, you betcha, but hain't ver sale. He joist dont look goot. I vont sell him ver money."

The trader protested: "I'm hurtin' for mules. I'm payin' ceiling prices. Mules have never been this high before and they never will be agin. You had better sell your mule while the sellin' is so good."

Hans reiterated his position: "Dot mule ist a vin mule. Only he joist dont look goot." The trader had heard about the idiosyncrasies of Hans and his way with English, so he stepped around the corner of the house to look at the mule just to be on the safe side. He thought the mule looked nice and fat, had a nice shine on its coat, and appeared to be lively. He returned to Hans and said: "Hans, that mule might not look good to you, but she looks damn good to me."

Then, almost as an afterthought, the trader decided that he had better depreciate the animal somewhat, just as a matter of good routine. "Of course, there's a little too much daylight under her, but I'm going to buy her anyway. I'll pay you $300 cash." Without hesitating, the trader counted out three hundred dollars. Hans eyes brightened at the sight of the money. His sales resistance completely broke down.

"Now," said the trader, "I want you to deliver that mule to my barn in Versailles." Hans nodded and the trader left. The next day, Hans delivered the mule as told. As the trader reached for the mule to lead it to a stall, he stopped in his tracks: "My God, Hans, this mule is stone blind." "Veil, I tolt you he vas a vine mule, but he joist don't look goot."

Sometimes the trader had pangs of conscience like the young trader who had sold a mean and dangerous mule to an old, bearded and tottering Mennonite farmer. The trader, in his eagerness to be rid of the troublemaker, had not bothered to warn the old-timer about the risks involved. For months, the trader was haunted by the fear that the mule would possibly kill or seriously injure his new owner. About a year later, the trader happened to drive by the old farmer's field. He couldn't believe his eyes. There he was plowing his field with this particular mule who was performing his duties in a most gentle and subdued manner.

Although many mule traders later became car dealers, one car dealer learned a hard lesson from trading with a mule farmer. A farmer came into the dealership and asked about the price of a new car. The dealer who was city bred and city raised immediately gave him the full treatment.

The farmer quickly came to the point. What was the price and would the dealer take a trade-in. The dealer gave the conventional price and indicated he was very interested in taking anything of value as a down payment. The farmer mentioned that he had two mules and both mules were heavy with foals and, since mules invariably have twins, this would mean that the dealer would very quickly have six mules. The farmer added that the price of mules in the market place was two hundred dollars. For bargain sake, the farmer would be content with $800 for the mules which would very quickly be worth $1200.

The dealer eagerly closed the deal. The farmer produced his two mules and the dealer put them in pasture just out of town. A few months later, the dealer made a trip to the farmer who was keeping his mules. Looking them over, the automobile dealer was very surprised. The farmer felt that he may have been at some fault in his caretaking. He asked the dealer what the trouble was. The auto man asked: "Where are the colts?" Sadly, he learned some mule biology but he had already flunked the test.

The smallest traders, and the ones with the least status, were the "nickle and dime traders." Mostly, they were vagabonds who passed in the night and were never seen again. Sometimes, however, they did stay in a particular locale permanently. They almost always demanded cash in payment, while the other traders would sell on time payment.

Sid Sunderman might be a composite picture of several small shady mule traders. Sid made a practice of buying mules on faith alone. He would write hot checks for their purchase and then race the mules to the nearest town auction and put them up for sale. Then he would take the money from the auction sale to cover the original hot checks.

There was hardly a session of the county court that convened without Sid's name on the docket. Either he was suing someone else or someone else was suing him. Sid did not win every case but often enough so that he came out ahead of the game. However, one time he came out on the short end. Sid had bought a sick mule, sick with pneumonia. Sid knew it and the seller knew it. But Sid thought he could make a fast dollar. He bought the mule for fifteen dollars. Then he called on the local rendering plant and told them he had a mule to sell them. The manager of the plant asked how much Sid wanted for the mule. Sid said fifty dollars. The manager laughed at Sid and said: "I'll just wait until tomorrow and get the mule for nothing." That night, the mule died and the carcass was sent to the rendering plant.

Nevertheless, Sid's reputation still remained relatively high. Not too long after the above incident, Sid was involved in a serious fight and lost one of his eyes. When a close German friend of Sid's learned of this tragedy, he shrugged off the incident by saying: "Dot fellow, Sid, see plenty mit von eye."

Because of their reputation, some traders had trouble with bankers and obtaining a line of credit. Most of the traders did not like to carry cash money on their person, so most of their purchases were made by check or notes on the local bank. Sometimes the bankers were overly skeptical about extending credit to the trader. Once a trader really "cussed out" a particular banker for his lack of trust and surliness. He closed the tirade by reminding the banker that there were far more bank presidents in the penitentiary than mule traders. In the end, the bank president conceded: "Your eloquence is very persuasive. Under the existing conditions, the least I can do is to cash your checks."

President Truman had a favorite mule trader story that he often told in front of his portrait wherein he was dressed in full Masonic regalia. One time a Catholic priest was driving through Georgia on a hot, dusty summer day. He decided to stop at a farm house to ask for a drink of water. He knocked on the door and when the lady answered, he asked her for a drink since it was so hot and dry. She looked at him carefully and then said: "Are you a Catholic priest?" He answered that he was. She became furious and told him to get off her property as quickly as he could.

As he turned and walked away, she reconsidered. "That's all you want, a glass of water?" "Yes, that's all I want. It is so hot and dusty and I had become very thirsty," said the priest.

"Well, I guess I can give you a drink as long as you promise that is all," She invited him into the hallway and went to get him a glass of ice water. As he stood there waiting, he looked into the living room and was astounded to see a big portrait of Pope Pius XII over the fireplace.

After he had drunk the water, he turned to leave. But, he couldn't leave without asking about the portrait. "Lady, please forgive me. I have to ask this question. You wouldn't have a thing to do with me because I am a Catholic priest, yet, over your fireplace you have this big portrait of the Pope Pius XII. How come?"

The lady was dumfounded. "Pope Pius XII. That lying mule trader told me it was Harry S. Truman in his Masonic regalia."

Despite whatever shortcomings the traders may have had, they added much humor and excitement to the affairs of many small towns. They were always interesting and provided challenges for the enterprising farmers and breeders. Because of their travels, they became acquainted with many people and learned how to get along with all kinds of personalities. They were fast talkers and persuasive. They had to be able to sell themselves as trustworthy. Is it any wonder then that many of them turned to politics at one point or another? Or to selling used cars?

Chapter Seven

Big Business in Mules

The biggest mule trader of all time was Ferdinand Lincoln Owen, simply known as Ferd Owen, Mule King. By the late 1940s, Ferd reckoned that he had traded at least a half million mules. An amazing accessory of this achievement was the fact that he could remember just about every mule and what he paid for it. And this was no trader exaggeration!

Frequently skeptics had challenged his memory of animals purchased and sold. They always lost their wager. His prodigious memory played a big part in his success. He didn't learn to read and write until Bertie, his wife, taught him. By then he was well established in the tradin' business. There was no question that his wife, Bertie, added to the efficiency and success of the business. She even helped to break the new purchases.

Like many traders, Ferd started buyin' and sellin' as a youngster. Also, like many young beginners, he got cheated a few times. His father made him absorb the hard lesson: "If you get skinned, learn to sit on the blister."

At the age of 15, Owen became a road trader or "gypsy" as he covered the Ozarks in a wagon and a string of animals tied behind. This experience provided a real test of business survival. As Ferd said, when you are poor, you can't afford to make a mistake. You have no margin to lose.

Moreover, being on the road alone could be dangerous. Ferd preferred to talk his way out of tight situations whenever possible. "I was always right handy with what I wanted to say, but sometimes words weren't enough. Once I was outside Eminence, Missouri, and a long lanky feller came along wanting to trade his mule for one of mine. We traded then and there. Fair Split. Later that day, that fella came back and said I had lied. 'That's impossible,' I told him, 'you never asked me a question.' He became more and more insulting so I finally hauled off and mite near broke his jaw. We were standing on a ridge top and he rolled ten or fifteen feet down into a creek.

"It was already late, so I set up camp close by. That night, the feller came back with a few friends. I could hear them coming through the brush so I looked around the wagon for something to defend myself. All I could find was a nice sharp meat cleaver. Then I steadied myself and yelled out: 'You boys are going to maul me, but before you do, I am going to get my share of fingers, hands and arms with this meat cleaver.' The bunch stopped in their tracks.

The defeated farmer muttered: 'He'll do it too.' The group cussed me out a little but they finally turned away.

"After that, me and the farmer became fast friends. I was tradin' over near Birch Tree when he was playing ball there. He called me over and I sat on the bench all through the game and afterwards drank beer with the entire team when the game was over."

By the age of 57 (b. 1891), Ferd Owen was acclaimed by Roger Butterfield in a *LIFE* magazine article "...as the biggest—and just about the smartest—dealer in America and, very likely, in the world. In 1946 he had sold 100,000 animals for a turnover of $7,500,000.

"Owen sells to Italy, France, Spain, Belgium and many other countries. He was the principal source of supply for UNRRA officials when they were restocking Poland, Yugoslavia and Greece with draft animals after World War II. He shipped 40,000 mules through UNRRA and established his own docks and yards in Savannah, Georgia, for that purpose.

"Inside the U.S., his shipments range from logging camps in Maine to the cotton fields of Texas, Mississippi and the Carolinas. He sells 'sugar mules' (tall, weighing 1100 pounds) in Louisiana, 'tobacco mules' (medium tall, 1000 pounds) in Georgia, 'banana mules' (small and wiry, 600 to 800 pounds) to the West Indies and Central America....He also supplies 'fancy' animals...for foxhunting to Virginia and Kentucky."

Without question, Mule King Owen had a kingdom. His main ministers, widely distributed geographically, were his seven brothers, innumerable cousins and in-laws. Brother Hazelton ("Has") was in Texarkana, Texas; brother Marvin in Meridian and Hattiesburg, Mississippi; brother Artemus Ward ("Art"), in Joplin, Missouri; nephew Wayne Owen in Nashville; and nephew "Odie" Owen in Memphis. Working together like an interlocking holding company, they controlled over half of the mule and horse trading in the country. They all acknowledged Ferd as the CEO and the spark that made the business go.

Another important part of Ferd Owen was pride and awareness of being an Ozarkian. He didn't try to pretend to be something else after he accumulated his fortune. Once a rich lady came up to Kansas City to buy some animals from Ferd. She had stopped in the Ozarks on her way up and she told Ferd that the Ozarkians down there were just plain stupid and lazy. Ferd laughed and then told her that half of those people were his kinfolks. He then proceeded to skin her alive in the tradin'. Afterwards, he thought that she might have a different idea about Ozarkians and their intelligence.

And of course, Ferd wore a big stickpin which consisted of a horseshoe of diamonds surrounding a small enameled mule's head with red ruby eyes. He called everyone "partner," and readily admitted that "tradin'" was always on his mind, "never did nothin' else." A close friend said "Everything Ferd has is for sale. For a long time, he couldn't keep a milk cow, a horse, a mule, whatever. Just as soon as a buyer would appear, the animal would go. He once bought a beautiful riding horse for Bertie, his wife, but sold it before he could get it to her. "I can't understand how Ferd has kept a wife as long as he has," a friend observed.

Before Ferd Owen reached the height of his profession, Guyton and Harrington had achieved colossal size and worldwide significance with their Mule and Horse Trading Company in Lathrop, Missouri. These two men came to Missouri from Alabama and Mississippi. Both men had been school teachers. Their company certainly rivaled the size of Ferd Owen's operations. For the five years of World War I, it was unparalleled in its buying and selling of mules and horses.

Thirty miles northeast of Kansas City, Lathrop, Missouri, existed as a typical small town. It became a most unusual place about the turn of the twentieth century. Foreign wars caused two mule booms which were truly amazing. As a result, Lathrop grew enormously. Today, Lathrop is once again a relatively inconspicuous small town.

But in the first twenty years of this century, Lathrop was an unbelievable place. At first, there were the British orders for mules needed in the Boer War; then there were more orders for World War I. The town's population became a polyglot group, a veritable Babel of tongues and races.

There were sepoys from India, Moslems from Jerusalem, Texas cowboys, French Canadians, British Army officers, and farmhands from Texas, Oklahoma, Kansas, Nebraska, and Iowa. Stories still circulate, especially about the sepoys, their eating habits and their unusual ability to run down and catch with their bare hands a Missouri jackrabbit. There were also elaborate fox hunts and parties for the English.

In the late 1890s, Guyton and Harrington was just one of a large number of mule companies in Kansas City. But then it acquired a monopoly contract to provide mules to the British Army. It grew to such a size that no other company could match it. The company expanded its holdings so that it reached all the way down to New Orleans from where the mules were shipped abroad. Hundreds of jobs were created for many different types of workers from wranglers to carpenters.

The Lathrop site grew to seven square miles where as many as 25,000 mules and horses could be handled daily. There were feeding depots and buying stations in East St. Louis, Nashville, Columbia, Tennessee, and Port Chalmette, Louisiana. The company simply dominated the mule market. The barns were record size. One hay shed measured 496 feet in length. The amount of hay and grain stored was beyond imagination. Daily, one hundred wagons hauled feed, and two hundred men were needed to feed and water the animals. Another hundred men handled the roundup activities and loading.

There was a constant labor shortage. Every hobo who wanted a job was handed a pitchfork and put to work. Over five hundred agents were contracted to scour the entire country for every serviceable mule and horse to be found. The company not only had its own buyers, but it served as a giant middleman for the other mule companies. The British would buy only from Guyton and Harrington, but other companies could get in the business by selling to Guyton and Harrington.

Strangely, the monopoly covered mules only. Other companies could sell horses directly to the British. Sparks and Company sold thousands of horses to England and thousands of mules and horses to the other allied countries. France entered the American market in 1915, and Italy soon followed. Maxwell and Crouch of St. Louis had a single order of 35,000 mules from the Italian government.

An army of mule traders covered the countryside looking for suitable mules. One of the best agents for Guyton and Harrington was Dave Baer of Belleville, Illinois, who became the company's chief representative in Illinois. He had complete freedom to buy mules wherever the sale was good. The company expected him to buy 200 mules a week and it would pay him $5 a head. Soon he was told to buy all he could. One day he bought 379 mules in Danville, Illinois;

another day, 450 in Lexington, Kentucky. In World War I, Dave bought over 100,000 mules and never had one of his purchases rejected by the company.

With such an overwhelming demand for mules from the foreign and domestic market, the price of mules soared. In 1916, a pair of three-year-olds sold for $1,000 in Kansas City. A yearling mule sold for $550. It is no wonder that farmers paid more and more attention to the "mule crop" and expanded its production. Some asserted the mule became another link in the chain that bound the United States to the Allied cause and weakened the midwestern isolationist position.

On the civilian front, traders often became the biggest business man in town. Maxwell and Crouch of St. Louis was incorporated and listed on the New York Stock Exchange. Banks in rural Missouri often listed more "paper" on mules than they did on real estate. Every village seemed to have a tradin' barn or two, and, on mule-tradin' day, these little towns were alive and doing a landslide business.

The roads in and out of Lathrop were pounded to a fine clay powder and clouds of dust announced the arrival of another large shipment of mules. There was constant activity. Three railroads ran hourly trains, and on certain days, as many freight cars were switched here as in Kansas City.

Girth Wilhoit, a foreman of the loading operations, recalled that 1550 mules could be loaded in an hour and ten minutes. Shipments were not by the carload, but by the trainload. At times, travel on the Lathrop streets became so hazardous and clogged, that farmers despaired of coming to town. Rain and mud made bad conditions even worse. Residents recalled the incessant activity and marvelled that it could increase month to month.

The town attracted horse and mule men, expert riders and drivers. Some observers thought that Lathrop had collected more knowledge and wisdom and experience in dealing with mules than any place or time in history.

Lathrop had its own rodeo everyday, in a manner of speaking. The English would accept as "broken" any animal that could be ridden down a twenty-five foot runway. Consequently, Guyton and Harrington found the best riders available to ensure the largest number of "broken" mules. Despite their skill and experience, some riders had great difficulty with some kickers and buckers.

The enormity of this wartime industry put "Missouri" mules in sharp focus and contributed to the practice of calling all mules Missouri mules. It also provided great business opportunities for many young, energetic businessmen.

In addition to these large enterprises, there were many individual traders, some of whom did a large volume of business and all of whom were colorful characters. The list would be long but two or three of them will illustrate their unique character.

Diamond Bill Hall came from Lancaster, Missouri which had become a wintering place for many circuses and sideshows, such as Howe's Great London Show, Yank Robinson Show, Walter L. Main Show, Buck Jones Show, Honest Bill Show, Atteberry Show, Campbell Show, and the Sells-Fleta Show. There were others as well. Bill Hall was mainly responsible for making Lancaster the circus capital of the world. Bill Hall the ringmaster and mulemaster!

At an early age, Diamond Bill wanted to be in a Wild West Show. He was fascinated by animals of all kinds, so it was easy for him to include mules in his menagerie. With all the exotic animals of the world in a small town in northern Missouri, one can understand why many people overlooked the fact that Diamond Bill was a leading mule trader in Missouri. When the St. Louis World's Fair decided to feature a mock-up of the Boer War, Bill Hall was called upon to furnish all the mules and horses for the attraction.

The Boer War had given Hall an entre to the African market. After this war, he began shipping one hundred mules to Capetown every three months. These shipments were always accompanied by young farmhands and how they relished "seeing the world." Eventually, Diamond Bill opened a sales barn in Capetown.

One can readily see that this man had grandiose dreams, but he often had the energy and ability to make them come true. Bill was a man of action who always seemed to know what to do in any emergency, whether it was a runaway elephant or mule. He could never decide which of the two animals was the most difficult to handle.

Hall applied his ringmanship to his mule business. He knew how to advertise and he would bill a town for a mule sale just as he might for a circus. A friend went to Cordon, Iowa to buy mules. The first thing he saw in Cordon was a huge lifesize picture of Bill Hall on one of the town's billboards. Below the picture was an announcement of the mule sale: "Buy one, Buy a hundred." People crowded the streets just as if a circus had come to town. And Bill would buy 100 to 200 mules a day.

Hall participated heavily in the mule boom of World War I. Many foreign buyers came to Lancaster to select their mules and horses. Apparently Diamond Bill sold to both the Allies and the Central Powers. In 1915, there was a newspaper story that Bill had completed a sale to Germany.

Tom Robnett, from Columbia, Missouri thought he was a big trader and quick to make a deal until he went to Lancaster to buy some mules from Bill Hall. When Tom arrived, he found out everything was free for a mule trader: hotel, meals, cigars, whiskey, and whatever else a man wanted. Tom went to Hall's farm and saw Hall out in the corral, knee deep in mud. Around him were elephants, mules, horses and cows. Hall was wearing a tall stove pipe hat, a large green scarf and tall hip boots.

Robnett never saw such activity. Hall was a dynamo giving orders every which way. Teams of men were unloading feed, driving mules, and watering the stock. Tom walked out to meet him but he didn't know if Hall was going to have time to talk to him. He always seemed to be talking to someone else.

Finally Robnett selected some mules he liked and shouted to Bill, "I'd like to buy some mules." Hardly looking at Tom, Hall replied: "All right, all right, cut one mule, cut a hundred, but hurry to it. What do you want to give me for them? They're worth $160. Cut as many as you like, one or a hundred." Tom suggested $140. "OK, OK, we'll split the difference. I'll take $150. Take as many as you like."

Tom couldn't believe how quickly it had happened. Bill said: "Take as many mules as you like. Go by the office and pick up a bill of sale. Leave your check or send it. It don't make no difference. The mules will be on their way to you tomorrow."

Tom managed to get to the office which was a sight in itself. It was one of the coaches from the Walter L. Main Show, the most elaborate railroad circus coach ever built. On top of it was a lifesized elephant made of wood. Tom paid for the mules, not knowing really which ones he had bought until he got home.

Bill Hall died in 1932. At the time of his death, his business amounted to very little. Mechanization had ruined his mule and horse operation. Radio and Movies seemed to hurt the circus. Today Lancaster lacks the zest and excitement of Bill Hall's day. It is quiet and small as it was before Diamond Bill Hall arrived.

Then there was another Bill, Bill McVean or Tipton, Missouri. Mr. Mac was a small dealer since he never sold more than a 100 mules a year nor had more than thirty in pasture. His knowledge, however, exceeded that of other traders with fifty times the yearly sales receipts. No one could pick a mule better than Bill. When he was so old that he had seen "five crops of the seventeen year locust," Bill could still size up a mule a hundred yards away more perceptively than a vet could after cutting him up. At least that is what the boys at the Tipton sales barn said.

Some said that he looked like Buffalo Bill. He was not a champion six-shooter, but he was champ of the country store tale and the victor at poolroom jest. One day a stranger asked him if he had ever farmed.

"Yep, I farmed nearly all my life. Never was much of a success but I kept at it. I'm an agriculturalist really, not a farmer. And there's a heap of difference. You see, a farmer has his holdings, his resources, in the country and his liabilities in town. On the other hand, an agriculturalist has his liabilities in the country and his assets in town."

When Bill was seventeen, his uncle asked him to take a carload of mules to the Memphis market. Bill could take along another carload of his own mules. Mules were the source of many different kinds of diversion. There was always the chance that once or twice during a season, a youngster would be asked to ride the mule train. Sometimes it even included a boat ride to foreign places.

On this occasion, Bill was off to Memphis for the first time. Once there, he was to sell the mules to a certain Mr. Martin, an acquaintance of Bill's uncle. Bill couldn't believe his good fortune. Mr. Martin offered $90 for each of Bill's small mules and $120 for his uncle's big mules. Bill had paid only $25 for his little mules and here he was getting more than three times as much. And to top off the deal, Mr. Martin agreed to pay the freight and feed bill for the shipment. Bill didn't realize how quickly one could be hooked onto tradin'.

Bill McVean was always attached to the truth. He wanted to be known as an honest dealer and fair. But it was a constant battle to keep one's reputation, especially when you had some no good animals to get rid of. Then it was hard not to conceal something and mislead a little bit. Once Bill was talking to a friend in a bar about a certain mule that had almost killed the friend. Evidently the mule had been extremely mean and uncontrollable. Bill told Oscar that the mule was now so gentle that Bill's daughter was riding him to school.

The friend looked at Bill and said: "You're a damn liar!"

Everyone at the bar stopped drinking and circled around to see what was going to happen. Bill took another drink, and, as unconcerned as he had been when he made the first remark, he answered: "Oscar, you are the first man I ever met to tell the truth about one of my lies."

"Mr. Mac" was a favorite character among many mule men in Missouri. They all seemed to have a favorite story about him. They respected his astuteness and his sense of proportion. He was content to be a small trader and stay within the bounds of his happiness.

Finally, there was Joe Kendig, a Pennsylvania Dutch mule trader. He was a favorite of Professor Jim Burkhart because Kendig's granddaughter attended Stephens College in Columbia, Missouri. Through her, Burkhart met some of the Kendig family.

Joe Kendig's father had become a trader before the Civil War over the disapproval of his Mennonite community. He was intended for the ministry as his father before him. To follow God's will one must make his living, preferably, from the soil, but certainly not through the exploitation of others in trade and commerce. But George Kendig wanted to be a trader and so he was excommunicated from his church.

Nevertheless, Mr. and Mrs. George Kendig continued to attend church services, and when they died, both were buried in consecrated ground within the church yard. This was a high tribute to his character and integrity.

George Kendig had started the practice of coming to Missouri and Kentucky to buy mules for the Mennonite farmers in York and Lancaster counties in Pennsylvania. He would usually buy six carloads at a time which would be about 150 mules. Along with the mules, he usually brought some negro slaves to help with the mules. Actually, he was providing them a way of escape to freedom.

Kendig was the first trader to introduce Missouri mules into York and Lancaster counties because he thought it would be cheaper to import them than to raise them at home. The Pennsylvania Dutch wanted young, fresh mules who could work hard. When these mules reached seven or eight years of age, they were sold down south where age didn't seem to be such a hindrance. And so the Kendig business grew. He brought in the young mules from Missouri and moved the older mules down south. He had his own triangular trade.

George Kendig also had a big family with six sons. They all became traders and located in Philadelphia, Baltimore, Norfolk and Richmond. The youngest, Joe Kendig, stayed home and worked with his father until 1899 when his father died and Joe took over the parent company at York, Pa. Together, the six sons formed a giant mule and horse syndicate. While each market was a completely independent and separate operation, the total business of the Kendig organization was large indeed.

Joe Kendig developed the York market until his sales exceeded those of any of his brothers. He would often have 800 or more mules on hand at one time. His barns were modelled after the big barns in St. Louis with wide alleyways.

The Pennsylvania Dutch farmers, for the most part, preferred the mule to the horse. Pound for pound, they argued, the mule was a better investment. He pulled better in the hot sun, ate less, had a certain hybrid vigor, was rarely ill, and held his soundness longer. Since they sold them at seven or eight years of age, and bought younger mules, it was said that a mule never died in York or Lancaster counties.

The Mennonites were very trustworthy people and so Joe Kendig had few worries about collecting on his sales. But they were shrewd and hard bargainers. They demanded value for their hard earned money. They often had their own ideas about a proper price for mules and would walk away if the price was too high.

Because of his integrity and long history of trading, Joe was able to develop a special relationship with one of the Mennonite ministers. This minister sometimes held church services in Kendig's barn. Since many Mennonites felt that ornate and expensive church buildings violated the very purpose of worship, the holding of religious services in barns was not uncommon.

This church leader also helped Joe with his mule sales. Joe made sure that the minister knew when and where the sales would be held. The minister would do the rest. He increased the publicity for the sale and also created the atmosphere of sanctioned recreation. Sometimes Joe sold a whole carload of mules in the church yard.

Drawing certain church members aside, the minister would say to them: "Your team is getting old now. You need a fresh team. Kendig has always treated us right. Think with him." Or the minister might have a prospective buyer to suggest in another part of the county. "Why don't you stop at this farm?" Or, "you can't go wrong talking to Harry Stemen."

Joe Kendig died in 1934 at the age of seventy-eight. He left a legacy of good will and friendship and a preference for mules among the Pennsylvania Dutch farmers that still continues. In 1954, at the Kansas City Royal, Peries Irving, one of the biggest mule raisers in Illinois, told Burkhart that his best market for mules was in York and

Lancaster counties. He had been selling to them since 1941.

Burkhart asked Irving why the Dutch preferred mules. The mule breeder grinned and answered that the Dutch regarded the mule as a test of strength, a challenge of wits, and match for their own stubbornness. The Dutch refused to give in. Moreover, the Dutch knew the indestructible qualities of the mule. They knew a good thing when they saw it and they couldn't pass up a bargain.

Chapter Eight

The Missouri Mule or Muletide in Missouri

Why should all mules be called "Missouri Mules"? Many farmers and breeders in other states, particularly Kentucky, Tennessee, Arkansas, and Texas, scoff at this name. They want recognition for their mules, some even want admission of superiority for their animals. The resentment and jealousy continue to the present day, long after the glory years of the mule.

To settle this question once and for all, the Chamber of Commerce in Benson, North Carolina, proposed a national mule race and invited all the state governors to send a mule entry. Thus it could be determined which state produced the champion mule.

However, Missouri Governor Warren Hearnes refused to be drawn into such a thinly disguised trap. Hearnes wrote the Benson Chamber of Commerce: "Dating back to pioneer days, it has been well established that Missouri mules are the finest, fastest, and hardest working of all mules and that, in truth, the mules located in any part of our nation properly should be described as Missouri Mules. Naturally, this means Missouri will be entitled to claim victory no matter which mule wins the race."

Sometimes the sinister slandering of the Missouri mule came from abroad. Paul J. Siemer reported in the *St. Louis Globe-Democrat* in 1976 that the African country of Ghana was shopping for 2,000 mules to haul its portable artillery and the shopping was being done in Switzerland. Pouring gasoline on the incipient fire, Raymond Gentinetta, a leading Swiss mule breeder, said that the Ghanian military men had "come to the right place if they were seeking the finest mules in the world. Our mules are the best in the world, the offspring of Jura mares and male Italian asses...unmatched in endurance, work performance and health."

Siemer wrote that Gentinetta's brash statement was "forty pounds of fertilizer" and that maybe Gentinetta was looking "for one swift kick in the Alps." Roger Conklin of Columbia, treasurer of the Missouri Hunting Mule Association (which doesn't hunt mules but hunts from mules) said: "I don't really see how these Swiss mules could be better...Not having seen their mules and all. But Missouri is known as the mule capital of the world. I think they're just blowin' their horn, personally."

Claude Adams from Lamar, Missouri, became a little excited by the challenge: "I doubt that very much...why I've never even seen a Switzerland mule."

U.S. Representative William L. Hungate, Democrat from Troy, Missouri, laughed: "Anybody that doesn't buy his mules in Missouri takes the chance of making an ass of himself."

Siemer gave the last shot to the Governor's office in Jefferson City. Writing for Governor Christopher Bond, the executive assistant, Ralph N. Smith said: "Well, I'll say this—if the Swiss mules are as stubborn as ours, the Ghanian army will not be able to move its artillery at all. Who knows? It might prevent a war."

The best explanation for the mule's identification with Missouri is the most obvious one. There was such a quantity of finely bred mules in Missouri that they became one of the state's most publicized products. At the Missouri State Fair, the winner of the "Mule Contest" was called the "World Champion Mule," and no one challenged this appellation for years.

Some years ago some Missourians wanted to change the seal of Missouri which features two bears. These true citizens wanted the bears to be replaced by mules. Unbelievably, the effort failed. The failure was comparable to Churchill losing his re-election bid in June, 1945, right at the end of World War II. How could the English voters reject him at the apex of his accomplishments for his country? How could Missourians reject the mule after all its accomplishments and honors for the state's name? Besides, the only bears in the state are in zoos.

How did all this mule business get started in Missouri? Great herds of mules from the Spanish border lands travelled to Missouri when the Santa Fe Trail was opened in the early 1820s. Not long after, jacks and mares were brought in from the East. Mules became big business and farmers throughout the state contributed their part in the growing enterprise. Being at the center of things geographically, many people poured through Missouri going in all kinds of direction. They needed transportation and mules were part of the answer to their needs.

After the Civil War, when the southern states were devastated and slow to achieving economic recovery, Missouri became the number one producer of this unique product. Used extensively before the Civil War, the mule was even more popular after the war. The southerners used them for all kinds of work and most of these mules came from Missouri. At the end of the nineteenth century, "in mules Missouri stood at the head, the only safe place." Missouri produced more mules annually than any other state.

The product became so renowned and commonplace that it became a very powerful symbol. Today's advertisers would probably refer to this phenomenon as "Mule Power". Like the present-day Golden Retreiver dog, the mule was and continues to be used to sell many different kinds of products because of positive image and popularity. For a long time, Borax used the 20 Mule Team picture to sell its products. Frankie Lane had a smash-hit recording of a song by that name.

In the early 1970s, Volkswagen used the mule in a wonderful advertisement. A weathered Ozark couple sat in front of their delapidated shack with junk all around but, in front of them, was a shiny new VW. The ad's caption said: "It seemed like the only thing to do when the mule died."

Hearing aid companies have used the picture of a mule and his big sensitive ears to sell their products. These companies boasted that science was finally catching up with the marvelous mule.

In the early 1990s, Jack Daniel's Whiskey used a picture of a farmer and his mule to sell their whiskey. This ad emphasized the company's stubbornness in sticking with their old tried and true method of distilling its whiskey.

In the 1994 Winter Olympics, a new event captured considerable attention, "Aerial Skiing." It is a wild and dangerous sport, some observers called it, "outrageous." One manuever which always attracted attention was the "Leroy." The rule book described it as a "Mule Kick in a Tip Cross Position." The book then identified the Mule Kick as a combination of the Side Kick and the Back Scratcher. Other official manuevers in Aerial Skiing are the Twister, Helicopter, Splitster, Spread Eagle, Iron Cross, Zudnick and Daffy. One can see why the mule would be a part of such a sporting event.

Yet another explanation for the mule's association with Missouri is the catchy alliteration of "Missouri Mule." Kentucky Mule, Texas Mule, or Illinois Mule just do not sound or look proper. Sometimes the simplest explanation is the best!

Few states have as much pride and braggadocio as Texas. It is especially nagging for Missourians to have a Texas braggart come to town and find nothing to admire and everything to insult. One such Texas provincial came to St. Joe, Missouri, and began to belittle Missouri's secular saint, Jesse James. Jesse still "lives in them parts" as Homer Croy put it in his book about Mr. James. After tolerating as much blasphemy as a mortal man could stand, one salty Missouri mule trader called a halt. "Listen Tex," he said, "You know what? Last week I shipped one of my inferior Missouri mules to Texas, and, in doing so, I raised the I.Q. of both states."

Similar in tone and twist was a riddle which made the rounds at the turn of the last century. The riddle asked: "Do you know why Missouri is first in mules and Minnesota is first in Swedes?" The answer: "Missouri got first choice." There was something mutually exclusive about Swedes and mules. A Swedish-American, living in Nebraska, acknowledged that when his parents come from Sweden to America, they first settled in Missouri. However, they soon discovered that there simply wasn't room in the state for both Swedes and mules, so the Swedes went further west. Naturally, this is how and why the United States expanded westward.

Many other riddles circulated beyond the borders of Missouri. This one would never have passed muster inside the state. "Do yu'al know why a mule sweats more behind his ears than anywhar else?" "Well, the reason bein' because thar's more of 'em thar than anywhar else."

The mule, in or out of almost any context, made for funny stories. The pastor of a church on the edge of town phoned the local board of health one day to ask that a dead mule be removed from the front of his church. The young clerk cheekily remarked: "I thought you clergyman took care of the dead." "We do," shot back the pastor, "but first we get in touch with the relatives."

Missouri mules were not only frequent ingredients in anecdotes and wisecracks, but they were also a basic part of folklore wisdom. Missouri lore swells at the seams with much homely cleverness pertaining to the mule. "Never bet on what a man can do, or, what a mule WILL do." "The best way to put a mule into his stall is to hire someone else to do it." Many years ago, a nameless Negro farmhand said: "The Missouri Mule don't kick according to no rule." "When a mule kicks, make sure that's where you was."

Once a farmhand was being interviewed for a job. The farmer asked him if he was familiar with mules. "No sir, nothin', I way too smart to be familiar with mules."

Stories persist as to why a certain twist of the Missouri River became known as "Jackass Bend," or, how "Walkenda Creek" came to be. Jackass Bend was christened in honor of an unfortunate jack who happened to topple off a steamboat at that particular point. The origin of "Walkendo Creek" is a bit more complicated. A Negro slave was driving a mule team across a stream and the mules balked. He exhorted them: "Walk in da creek; go on, walk in da mud, walk in da, walk in da.d....walkenda creek."

But to get back to our main discussion, how did the mule come to Missouri and how did all mules come to be Missouri mules? It is sort of like all gelatins being called JELLO, or all paper tissues becoming KLEENEX. Only it's different.

Missouri is in the middle of everything, halfway between Canada and Mexico, and between the Atlantic and the Pacific. Missouri is the "Gateway to the West," or the "Mother of the West," whichever one preferred.

The Santa Fe Trail began in Missouri and it carried millions of people westward besides many other things. This trail brought thousands of Spanish mules into Missouri, both pack and dray animals. However, the Spanish mule proved inadequate for the hard, heavy, endless labor of the midwestern, Pennsylvanian, and Southern farms and the frontier freighting. The Spanish or Santa Fe mule weighed about 650 pounds which was far too light for the new freighting wagons and their 5,000 pounds of cargo. From these necessities, the Missouri mule was invented.

It may be a surprise to many historians even, but George Washington played a crucial role in this invention. In addition to being the Father of the United States, he is also known as the father of the American Mule Industry. Being a farmer, in addition to being a soldier, Washington needed big strong work animals. After considerable manuevering, Washington was able to persuade the King of Spain to give the Virginian a fine jack and two jennets. The jack was named, Royal Gift. Not long afterward, General Lafayette gave Washington another jack and two jennets from the Isle of Malta.

Washington then placed an ad in the MARYLAND JOURNAL and THE BALTIMORE ADVERTISER in 1788 which read in part: "Royal Gift and the Knight of Malta, two valuable imported jackasses, will cover mares and jennets at Mt. Vernon the ensuing spring for three guineas. The first jack is of the most valuable race in the kingdom of Spain; the other is of the best breed in Malta. Royal Gift, now six years old, has increased in size since he covered last season, and not a jenny, and hardly a mare to which he went, missed. The Knight of Malta will be four years old this spring, about 14 hands high, most beautifully formed and extremely light, active and sprightly. The two jacks seem as if designed for different purposes, but equally valuable: the first by his weight and strength to get mules for plow and heavy draught; the other by his activity and sprightliness for quicker movement.

By crossing the Spanish and Maltese ass families, LLoyd Linford thought Washington obtained exceptionally good seed stock to power the mule business forward. From this famous cross, Washington obtained his famous jack, Compound, who some consider to be the father of the American mule population. Because of Washington's prestige, and because of his good judgment, many jacks and jennets were to be imported from Spain, Malta, Majorca, France and other European locations to improve the American mule stock. One should also note a pre-eminent role played by Henry Clay, a few decades after Washington, in this drama.

By the middle of the nineteenth century, many imported jacks were being widely used. The Andalusian, Catalonian and Maltese jacks were in high demand. But, eventually, the best and most sought after jack came from France, from Poitou. Frank C. Mills thought the Poitou was the most perfectly formed of all the imported jacks; not so tall as the Majorca, but more powerful for his inches, with greater weight, more bone and superior muscle.

The Poitou jacks were expensive, costing often as much as $3,000. But their mules were unequaled and sold from fifty to one hundred per cent higher. The breeders of the Poitou had a stud book for the record of their stock, so there can no mistake as to purity from an early date. Their mules were less liable to disease, hardier, longer-lived and stronger than other mules. They also consumed less food.

The demand for the Poitou was high because of all these good qualities. In France, a special committee oversaw the registration of each animal to make sure of continuing quality. The high standards paid good dividends. In 1866, Poitou, about the size of an American county, produced 50,000 mules from their jacks. Frank C. Mills said the industry in Poitou was without equal in agriculture.

Pictures of the Poitou jacks are interesting. Their hair is exceedingly long and shaggy which appears unattractive at first. They are coal black with white points, range in height between 14 and 15 hands, and are immense in the size of their knees, hock, belt and length of ears. But their biggest and most important asset was the mules they produced. These mules were without peer as workers. General Charles DeGaulle regarded them as one of France's greatest treasures.

By using such good jacks along with high quality mares, Missouri achieved unquestioned supremacy in both quality and quantity of mules after the Civil for about a thirty or forty year period. Missouri Mules dominated the competition at the turn of the century at the great World Fairs in Chicago, St. Louis, San Francisco and Seattle. At the St. Louis Fair, one Missouri raiser, William Elgin, won so many prizes with his mules that when the checks began to arrive he thought a mistake had been made and actually sent back some of the prize money.

Not only did Missouri dominate in mules, the state also led the field in quality jacks. This great accomplishment was due to the genius of a special person, Colonel L.M. Monsees of Smithton, Missouri. His skill and demand for perfection created a line of champion jacks which lasted close to sixty years. His accomplishments at his Limestone Valley Farm are simply marvelous. At the St. Louis Fair, he won a total of 72 ribbons on thirty head of animals and was restricted to two entries in each class or he could have won more prizes.

At the Panama-Pacific Exposition in San Francisco in 1915, he won 66 ribbons on fourteen head of animals and he was not entered in three classes. In these two expositions, he won more prizes than all other exhibitors put together. From 1880 to 1910, Monsees sold over a million dollars worth of jacks and jennets. He started as a young boy by buying his first animal for two pocket knives, a pistol and $4.00.

During the twenties and thirties, Missouri agriculture experienced the depression along with all the other farmers. Mechanization and falling farm prices caused extreme readjustments and hardships. Interestingly, one of the most successful crops was the mule crop. A young mule would sell for $100 or $125 while a milk cow would bring only $10. Often the mule would outsell a horse by 10 to 20 per cent. If a farmer produced 10 or so mules, it could be his biggest source of income. Land sold for $1 or $2 an acre. Thus the sale of one mule could produce enough money to buy a small farm.

Mules served round the world in World War II, appearing in 10 different military theatres of operation. Burma and Italy were their principal areas. The Jeep and other mechanized equipment won great acclaim, but there were certain locales that this modern equipment could not handle. Such were the mountains of Italy and Burma and they provided yet another opportunity for the mule to prove its usefulness and sturdiness.

Certainly the story of the Missouri mule was a story with a kick in it. This Missouri outlaw could knock a hole in a two foot wall, and stand on his head and kick at the sky. He could chill the spine of the toughest muleskinner with his display of temper. The large barns, which mule barons built to house these critters until they were sold, had windows the size of a ray of sunlight. Stockmen felt that the Missouri mule was less lethal in a dimly lit enclosure than in a well lighted one.

Missouri mule buyers, out of respect, quickly learned to take off the shoes of newly acquired mules. A barefoot mule could kick just as hard as a mule with shoes on, but even a glancing blow from a shod mule was dangerous. To this very day, the railroads refuse to ship a Missouri mule with shoes on.

The growth of America can be told in part in terms of mules. Mules were used for every purpose imaginable. They helped build the railroads, logged the forests, plowed the fields, planted and harvested the crops, powered the early reapers and combines. They turned the grist mills, built the roadways, and forced the sugar out of the sugar cane. They groaned and sweated and kicked, but they did not stop. The penetration of American democracy into distant cultures was often accomplished by the adaptable mule, an able representative of such a highly individualized system of government and economy.

On the occasion of President Harry S Truman's inauguration in 1948, he requested a team of four mules and a wagon to be in the parade. Very appropriately, Claude Adams, a man from Lamar, Missouri, Truman's birthplace, and Ed Knell of Carthage supplied the rig requested. The Missouri mules somehow sensed the honor bestowed on them and acted accordingly as they pulled the families of these two men down the parade route.

However, the two men reversed the roles and acted in a very mulish manner. Beforehand, they had agreed to split the driving distance fifty-fifty. As they approached a large group of photographers, Knell was driving as it had been agreed. But Adams wanted his picture taken with the reins in his hands, so he proceeded to try to wrestle the reins from Knell. A fight ensued, a lifelong friendship and business partnership dissolved, and they never spoke to one another again.

The Truman parade reminded some people of a similar event when Champ Clark became Speaker of the House. Clark's friends decided a special parade was required for this occasion. Only this time, Clark actually rode down Pennsylvania Avenue in a carriage pulled by two Missouri mules, "Belle of Pike," and "Belle of Callaway." This parade was a glorious success and everyone behaved perfectly from top to bottom.

After Truman left the presidency, he attended the State Fair one year in Sedalia. After the mule contest, Truman was photographed with the two World Champion mules from Missouri. Later, when the president was given a enlarged copy of this photograph, he was elated. At the presentation, he said he couldn't wait to show it to his brother Vivian. Truman displayed this picture prominently in his Independence Library.

The most enjoyable conclusion to this debate would be the "Missouri Mule Bread" recipe of Kenneth Harris of Macon, Missouri. The ingredients are: 2 cups of warm water, 1 package of dry yeast, 1 half teaspoon salt, 5 tablespoons sugar, 1 tablespoon cinnamon, 3 tablespoons wild cherry jello, 1 half cup Crisco oil. Mix well.

To the above add 6 cups all purpose white flour, mix and knead well until proper consistency—let rise at room temperature until this dough has doubled its orginal capacity—now make this smart alec dough into rolls or loaves and place into well greased pans or bowls and make it again double its capacity (a few marks with a fork before it starts rising the second time will give it extra charm, like maybe a varmint had run over it). When dough has doubled the second time, put into 325 degree oven and gestation should be in about 25 to 30 minutes. Be sure and keep the oven door propped shut with a chunk of buckeye fire place wood.

—— Chapter Nine ——

Pack Mules and Wagon Mules

When man has back-breakin work to do, he looks for his mule.

Mule proverb.

"Mules? Pardner, I want you to remember that God made mules on purpose!"

Tom Moore, Army packmaster.

From earliest times, humans have used the ass and its offspring to do much of the heavy work which exceeds the strength of man. Thus the pack animal appeared frequently in Ancient and Biblical history and many different animals were employed as beasts of burden.

Spain gave the enterprise a pronounced Latin accent and brought it to a new crest of accomplishment and glory. Queen Isabella had organized the largest pack train in history in one of her military campaigns. This train included 15,000 mules. Such Spanish organizational skill and ingenuity were extremely useful in claiming colonies and wealth in Mexico, Peru and other parts of the New World. Long pack trains carried the new found wealth from the inner territories to the coasts for shipment to the mother country.

But Spain and her colonies were not unique in their use of the pack mule and other animals. In English North American colonies, virtually all land traffic consisted of pack trains as late as 1790 when the United States was being created. Packers and caravan drivers contracted to move supplies, equipment and people from the established eastern communities to the various and scattered frontier outposts.

Pack trains provided the only means of shipping goods from Philadelphia to Pittsburgh in the 1780s. The Pack Train drivers were a powerful pressure group that tried to prevent the construction of wagon roads and canals.

Some historians have speculated that the pack train or the absence of another system of freight transportation helped cause the Whiskey Rebellion in Western Pennsylvania during Washington's presidency. The farmers could not ship cheaply and quickly their grain over the mountains to the seacoast.

Rather than ship the bulk grain, they distilled their corn into whiskey and brandy and sent it over the mountains on pack animals. The mule or horse could carry sixteen gallons. Some packed the liquor in boots, and thus the term, bootlegger. The new federal excise tax angered the western farmers and helped spark the insurrection that every student smilingly learned as the "Whiskey Revolution."

Although the New World employed many different pack animals such as horses, asses, burros, llamas, camels, elephants (remember the King of Siam's offer to President Lincoln), and dogs, the mule became the outstanding favorite. At first, it was the Mexican mule. Being small, it was easier to load and to handle. But in the open plains, the Mexican Mule was gradually replaced by the American Mule which most often came from Missouri.

The mule's sure footedness, tough hide and hoofs, scantier appetite gave this accident of nature an advantage over these other thoroughbreds. Some entrepreneurs in the 1850s thought that this was an ideal situation for introducing the camel since this animal could carry much larger and heavier loads. A camel can carry 800 to 1,000 pounds whereas a mule or horse would carry only 250 to 350 pounds. But the New World culture would not tolerate this mid-eastern contrivance and it disappeared after brief experimentation.

The shippers, packers and drivers had to pay close attention to what mules they used. The experienced hands often cited the old Etruscan proverb pertaining to the selection of a wife: "Close your eyes and put your trust in God;." Other more pragmatic business experts looked for sturdy legs, sure footedness, muscles, bright-eyes, sharp teeth (indicator of age), swishy tail and sound skin. In other words, the mule should be tough, strong, healthy and spirited. (Jay Monaghan, editor—*The Book of the American West*).

The veteran muleteer learned that he had to become intimately acquainted with the mule to get him to perform. This meant paying very close attention to his welfare. Most observers admitted that Mexicans made better muleteers because they understood the mule better and the mule understood the Mexican better. The Mexicans also seemed to have more patience so as to understand and endure the art of packing and unpacking a mule. W.A. Ferris, a seasoned Rocky Mountain traveler and philosopher, described the pack mules as infernal machines meant to do harm to the handlers. The beasts would bite, kick or step on the packer's feet. If one did manage to tie the load, the devil's helper would then shake violently so as to spill everything on the ground. The varmit's last trick would be to refuse to move if all other procedures failed. Their imagination seemed to have no end in making the packer's life miserable.

In addition to the needed forbearance, the Mexican muleteer brought a gay and carefree dress. They wore huge sombreros, colorful serapes, bright ribbons, sparkling spurs, and a brightly colored sash which often contained their insignia. They also carried a long bowie knife, pistol and lasso. And always there was the inevitable cigarette, dangling from sun parched lips. The English, French, Irish and German Americans found this ambiance difficult to emulate.

Considerable inventiveness was required in this contest between mule and man. Some packers found that the mule had to be blindfolded before he could be loaded. This trick provided man a major advantage in the mule battle.

All kinds of saddles and harnesses were invented to carry the freight or passengers. Different types of cargo required different saddles. When properly done, the mule could carry two to four hundred pounds, with the average load about 250. But "properly" meant that the mule could not feel mistreated. If the mule felt mistreated, hardly any saddle or harness arrangement or knot would hold the load in place. The mule could be creative in finding ways to "unload."

One critical discovery in the packing business was the recognition of the mule's affection for white mares. This mare attachment happened quickly and turned the mule into complete subservience, or almost so. The muleskinner learned that if he attached a bell to a mare's neck, the mule would follow without complaint as long as he could hear the bell. This insight meant that many fewer men were required to keep a train moving.

The bell mare really was a revolutionary invention because there had never been a successful way to tether mules together into a pack line. Four or five could be tied together and led by a muleskinner but even this arrangement did not work very well. With the bell mare, the train could be quite long. As long as the last mule could hear the bell he would follow along content as could be. Sometimes such a line could extend for 100 mules.

Even when the train stopped and the animals were unloaded and set free, the mules would all stay close by the mare with real affection in their eyes. One nameless poet wrote: "Behind the white bell mare, the endless train."

Without the bell mare, havoc and confusion resulted. Captain R. G. Carter described an attempt to let a pack herd officer lead the mules rather than the bell mare. It did not work. The mules crowded the trail and refused to string out. They became frightened at the least disturbance. Within ten minutes, utter confusion had thrown the mules into an indescribable mass. Before long soldiers were going in every direction trying to recapture the scattered workers. The men were overcome by the heat of the chase and sun and one officer passed out.

Pack trains developed their own ritual and routine but there were many similar procedures. The packing took place before sunrise so that the train could begin moving by sunrise. There would be a mid-day break for resting, watering and feeding. Then the march would resume until darkness. The work was long, hard and trying.

The skill of a good pack train manager was incredible. It was said that a seasoned muleskinner could take a grand piano over the Rockies "without losing a key or dropping a pitch." Of course the mule made his contribution to this achievement. One mule is said to have transported a pool table into Central City, Colorado. The legs of this table extended beyond the mule's head and tail. It did not touch the ground unless the animal stopped and squatted. Needless to say, this particular mule, being a sensible creature, proceeded to do just that from time to time. But the billiard table arrived at the mining camp in one piece, but it had several bowling alley groves running in all directions through the playing surface.

On another occasion, a mule pack train carried a load with built in mule obsolescence from at least two angles. Three hundred and fifty mules in a single train carried a mile long steel cable which was one and three quarters of an inch thick from Denver to Tellridge. The cable became an aerial tramway which then eliminated the need for pack transportation over the most difficult terrain in that part of the Rockies.

There seemed to be no end to the list of items which the pack trains took into the remote mountain reaches. One writer said that the mule was so "clothed upon" by his load that he was often invisible underneath it all. They carried sacks of flour, kegs of whiskey, bags of beans, buggies, tables, plows, printing presses, pianos, and iron safes.

J. W. Vaughan reported that "quicksilver" was the hardest of all to pack. The iron flasks contained ninety pounds of quicksilver, and the motion of the mules caused the metal to shift back and forth. In order to prevent injury to the mules, the packers learned to top off the flasks with water so there was no room left for shifting. As an additional precaution, the two flasks packed on each side of the mule were fastened in board frames.

The most obvious disadvantage of the pack train was the daily packing and unpacking of the cargo. In addition to being time consuming, it was dangerous, and it was a job requiring skill and patience as mentioned above. There seemed no end to the guile and devilment which the mule could invent.

One of his favorite ploys was inhaling while his load was being cinched. He would fill his body with air as if he were a dirigible. The amateur would have pity on the mule and not want to make the cinch too tight as to hurt the animal. There was nothing that the mule loved better than to be pitied. He took full advantage of such a situation. After the belt was fastened, the mule would exhale allowing his chest to return to normal size. The result was absolute chaos as the pack saddle slipped around to the belly side and all the paraphanalia would scatter on the ground.

One greenhorn had no sooner released his hands from the belt than the mule shook himself and sprang into action with a vigor that vibrated like an earthquake from his head to his stiffened tail. Not content with dumping the load on the ground, the mule commenced to prance stifflegged on all the equipment. When the novice tried to seize the halter and end the caper, the mule stood upright on his hind legs and began boxing and throwing lethal punches at his tormenter. At this point, a Missourian came along and took charge of the mule. The Show-Me citizen stuck one leg into the mule's side and pulled the cinch band until he almost cut the mule in two pieces. The mule knew he had met his master and quietly performed his duties.

As mentioned above, the pack train appeared early in history. In America, a high point of its development and use was in the Gold Rush Era in California. The mule pack train was often the only lifeline between river ports and mining locations. Mules have no equal in mountain passes and trails. They were so admirably suited for traversing the narrow pathways of the Sierra Nevadas that they were dubbed the "Clipper Ships of the mountains." Their tough skin was a big asset in the blinding rain, sleet and snow, as well as the blistering heat of the summer.

For a number of years, the only place many Americans knew in California was San Francisco. Everything was sent to this location and then somehow found its way to the correct person in the countryside. Sometimes this countryside extended long distances. For this reason many express companies came into existence to facilitate delivery. Only gradually did other locations come to be used such as Stockton, Sacramento and Marysville.

One packer who became quite successful in this new express business was a woman, Olga Schaaf. Elvon L. Howe called her a "Lady Jack Whacker," who would deliver supplies in places where men would refuse to go. The men were appalled by her "stupendous labor and personal risk." Her first contract was to take supplies into a mining area fittingly called, Neglected.

While the packer's life was harsh, it is noteworthy that the first California express packer was a "dropout" from mining. Because of his frail physique, Alexander H. Todd left the mines to start his own mule express company to carry mail to some 2,000 miners at a charge of $2.50 a letter. He carried the mail from San Francisco to the mining communities and increased his profit by carrying gold from the miners to the San Francisco mining houses for a charge of 5% of the gold's value.

Business was so good that more and more miners took up the mule packing business. One of the more famous express company operators was Daniel Dancer. He pushed long pack trains of a hundred and fifty mules to the high ridges of north Yuba. Over the years, his huge trains carried everything and anything. Nothing was too big or too small. He had a matchless record for never losing a load.

Years after when roads connected the larger mining centers to the coast, winter snows would often blockade the roads for all but an occasional mule train. In the northern regions of California, the mule express was the sole means of freighting well into the 1860s.

A much publicized pack train involved the taking of President Chester Arthur to Yellowstone Park. The train consisted of 400 mules who carried every conceivable implement and accoutrement which would make the trip enjoyable for the President. The description of the expedition would have provided excellent matter for an investigative reporter looking for a political story.

Despite all its success for such a long time, the pack train could not dominate the freighting business forever. Eventually road building and better wagon technology would cause the decline of the pack trains. This did not mean the demise of the mule. He was simply reprogrammed for a new job which was just as demanding physically. Later, after the Civil War, General Crook would resurrect the "pack mule" and elevate "pack training" to a highly specialized science.

As the wagon trains became more prevalent, the mule simply changed his job classification to wagon train employee. The number of mules hitched to a wagon varied from two to twenty, with a six mule team being very popular. A six mule team and a good wagon could carry more cargo than a 30 mule pack train. Moreover, the wagon didn't have to be loaded and unloaded twice a day. This fact removed the most hazardous feature of packing.

The technological shift to wagons occurred west of the Mississippi during the 1820s as the Santa Fe Trail and the Overland Trail developed greater and greater travel. Gradually St. Louis became a central location for many new companies producing bigger and better wagons. The "Murphy" wagon gained wide popularity and it proved to be very sturdy and durable. Joseph Murphy was a colorful figure who knew how to market as well as produce his product. Other outstanding wagons made in St. Louis had the interesting names of Luedinghaus and Espenschied. It was certainly one of the prominent "growth industries" of the time. The competition caused constant improvement and variety to serve the many needs of the travellers.

Because of its strategic position on the map, Missouri has long been a dominant transportation center, whether it is pack trains, wagon trains, railroads, automobiles, airplanes or space vehicles.

The use of bigger and heavier wagons also caused a shift in the making of the mule. The pack mule had been generally small, and this size was appropriate for small loads and travel in the mountains. But the long trek across the prairie and the bigger and heavier wagons required a larger and stronger mule. Thus the Spanish Mule gave way to the Missouri Mule. Big draft mares were matched with bigger and stronger jacks to produce big, strong, and splendid draft mules. These mules would be 15 to 16 hands and weigh 1200 to 1400 pounds. Sometimes the mule would be 18 to 19 hands and weigh 2000 pounds but this size was exceptional.

Considerable argument developed over the merits of the mule compared to the ox and horse. The ox was considerably cheaper but slower. They also performed better on snow and ice. Another major advantage for the ox was that he made a better source of food if he should be badly injured and had to be killed. The horse was generally faster but was not as durable as the mule or ox. The horse was also more expensive to feed and to shoe. All three animals were popular and used in great numbers.

The most famous and publicized wagon train operation became the Twenty Mule Teams of Death Valley which transported the desert borax. Television drama and Frankie Lane's song have made it immortal.

The borax wagons were unbelievably large. The rear wheels were seven feet in diameter, the front five feet. The steel tire was eight inches wide and one inch thick. These tires would weigh between 600 and 1,000 pounds and require at least six men to retire a wheel. The wagon bed was 16 feet long, four wide, and six deep. Two such wagons were hitched together with each carrying a ten ton load, which is almost the equivalent of a loaded railroad boxcar.

There were ten of these wagons in operation in the 1880s without a single breakdown. These monsters were pulled by a twenty mule team. Loaded, the train would travel 15 to 17 miles a day; unloaded, 22 miles. The round-trip was 330 miles.

The summer months were so hot that work was suspended from the middle of June to the middle of September. The mules must have thought these monsters were diabolic in origin. Twenty mule teams had been used before in history, but Harold O. Weight said that such teams were perfected in Death Valley's haul through hell. Calling it the Devil's golf course seemed to make light of how terrible and terrifying the terrain actually was.

By the end of 1858, there were six postal lines across the West. Two of them went south of border, one through Mexico and the other through Panama. The central route which started in Independence, Missouri and ran to Placerville, California by way of Salt Lake City required a thirty-eight day schedule. The Butterfield route began in St. Louis and ran to San Francisco by way of El Paso. It required twenty-five days. Le Roy R. Hafen has written an interesting account of the Overland Mail from 1849 to 1869.

Before the Civil War, the fastest freight train between St. Joseph, Missouri and Denver took twenty one days. It was a light train consisting of ten wagons and four mules to a wagon. This trip usually took six to eight weeks.

The fastest freighter on the Santa Fe Trail was a French Canadian, Francois Xavier Aubry. He set many records between Independence, Missouri, and Santa Fe. He was known as the "Skimmer of the Plains" as he seemed to fly over the distance. He preferred to use mules over oxen because of the greater speed.

One of the largest freighting companies in the West was the "Empire on Wheels" of Russell, Majors and Waddell. At one time the company owned or leased 15,000 mules, 50,000 oxen and "acres and acres of wagons, axel trees, wagon tongues and other equipment. Alexander Majors probably was the driving force behind the company's success. He initiated a humanized system of work which anticipated the scientific method of Taylorism but without its depersonalization.

Majors timed his muleskinners and bullwackers and trained them to yolk and hitch twelve oxen and have them ready for the trail within sixteen minutes. He had a printed manual containing job descriptions, work requirements, and the rules and regulations of the road. Each teamster was given two pistols, a rifle, and a bible. The teamster was asked to take an oath that he would not drink, gamble, swear, travel on Sunday or be cruel to animals. Buffalo Bill skoffed at such nonsense: "Majors might as well as read the Riot Act to a herd of stampeding buffaloes."

On one occasion, Majors refused to locate in Nebraska City, Nebraska, until the town dehydrated itself and became as dry as buffalo chips. Actually, Majors was not a fanatic about anything. He simply felt that the men who signed the employment pledge would be more dependable and productive.

When Majors's partner, William Russell, was under attack for collusion with the Secretary of War, John B. Floyd, and was accused of using the government's Indian Trust Bonds for loan collateral, an article in the New York Post mocked Majors's piety. Missouri newspapers staunchly defended Majors in insisting that his religion was not a proper subject for jest or ridicule. The Western Journal of Commerce in Kansas City speculated what could happen if the New York Post ridiculed Majors in front of his teamsters. "They would be with a Bible like a Quaker is with his coat." A proverbial Quaker, irritated beyond his self-control, finally took off his coat, laid it aside, and said to the coat: "Lie there, Quaker, while I give this fellow the thrashing he deserves."

Majors also is credited with devising the "Ecclesiastical Kiss." While visiting a friend, a small town minister, Majors greeted the minister's attractive wife and daughters with a kiss. The minister was taken back at the spontaneous show of affection, but Majors explained that the Bible admonishes all to "salute thy brother." Majors interpreted this passage to include sisters and the biblical salutation included the kiss.

Just as soon as Majors finished his interesting biblical exegesis, a doddering, old woman, withered and wrinkled, came by. The minister turned to Alex and said: "She is a sister of the church. Do you Christian duty." Majors did.

A revival meeting was in progress and Alex Majors became the star of the fellowship. His "Ecclesiastical Kiss" was so popular that the other churches spread the vicious rumor that perhaps the "kiss" was not all that spiritual. The revival meeting had to be broken up.

Historians generally agree that Majors was "kept in the dark" regarding the devious and illicit activities of his partner, William Russell. Russell, in fact, wrote to the third partner, William Waddell, urging him not to reveal certain shady business transactions to Alex Majors. Majors's uncompromising honesty is further confirmed by his insistence that all his assets be liquidated to satisfy the claims on the firm by its creditors.

Completely insolvent, Majors began anew in freighting and mining in Colorado, but was never successful. Forty years later, Buffalo Bill Cody, who had worked for Russell, Majors, and Waddell, found Majors almost destitute living in very poor circumstances in Denver. Cody found an editor, wrote the preface, and paid the cost for the publication of Majors's autobiography: My Seventy Years on the Frontier.

Just before the company of Russell, Majors, and Waddell folded, an exciting event occurred which became known throughout the West. And eastern bound stage roared into Bent's Fort in Colorado. The driver shouted that the firm of Russell, Majors and Waddell had gone bankrupt. John Campbell and Upton Hays were hardly disinterested bystanders since they were holding a draft of credit for $60,000 on the giant freighting company. Unless the draft could be cashed before the news of the collapse reached Kansas City, the $60,000 would be lost and Campbell and Hays would be in serious trouble. These circumstances caused one of the longest and fastest races on record.

Upton Hays, the grandson of Daniel Boone, agreed to race the stage to Kansas City and cash the drafts while they were still redeemable. To make the marathon run, Hays chose a sturdy mule named Sam. Kansas City was 620 miles away. The stage stopped at rest stations every 100 miles and changed teams even more frequently. Hays paused only momemtarily and rode the same mount all the way. When exhausted to the point of swaying in the saddle and unable to hold the reins, Hays dismounted and caught short snatches of sleep. The mule grazed a few feet nearby, hobbled to Hays's wrist.

On and on they went toward Kansas City. Hays rode his mule 620 miles in five days and 18 hours. He beat the stage and arrived before the news of the bankruptcy reached Kansas City. Hays cashed the drafts, and saved himself and his partner, John Campbell, from possible bankruptcy.

Sam, the racing mule, became the Eighth Wonder of the World. When Judge John C. Guage arrived in Kansas City in 1859, he noted that the newspapers were carrying more news about Sam's feat than any other topic. Judge Guage heard and read so much about Sam during his first week in town that he made a special trip out to John Campbell's place to see the mule and talk to it. Guage said: "I felt quite famous myself."

There is still today considerable historical argument over the authenticity of this event. Truly it would have been an incredible ride. The idea of a single mule running 620 miles in less than six days defies belief. Some parts of the story are verifiable and others are not. Russell, Majors, and Waddell officially declared bankruptcy in 1862, not 1859. The firm, however, was in serious financial trouble beginning in late 1858 when the military refused to compensate the company for losses suffered in the Utah War.

Arguing convincingly for the authenticity of the mule race are the character and reputation of John Campbell and Upton Hays. The prominent Campbell street in Kansas City is named for him, as well as Charlotte street for his wife. Upton Hays became involved in the Civil War as a Confederate Colonel in the Second Missouri Confederate Cavalry and was killed in a cavalry charge at the battle of Newtonia in September, 1862. In his obituary, there was one brief line that could have referred to his outstanding race: "Perhaps no finer horseman ever rode hard over the prairies." Here again, the poor mule, Sam, was cheated out of immortality by his cousin, the horse.

Hays is buried at the corner of Troost and 31st Street in Kansas City, Missouri, in a little known Confederate Cemetery with the quaint name of "Self Cemetery."

There are so many facets to the western expansion that take on gigantic proportions. Present-day Americans have to marvel at the determination of the western pioneers as they moved across the plains and mountains to the west coast. The people and their animals were made of stern stuff to endure. Thomas Jefferson had thought the vast western acreage would allow 1200 years of gradual development.

Chapter Ten

Muleskinners

"It takes more ability to be a muleskinner than it takes to be a member of Congress."

Vice President of the United States,
Schuyler Colfax.

The muleskinners held a lofty position in the western hierarchy. Contemporary television and films have exalted the sheriff, the cowboy or the wily scout and ignored for the most part the unique contribution of the muleteer. This oversight is interesting because some of the muleskinners had illustrious reputations and respect in addition to colorful personalities. Raw-boned, leather tanned by the sun and wind, he was the epitome of courage. It had to be so. Danger was his business. Indians, bandits, weather and terrain often embattled the muleskinner. And, of course, there was always the mule to hold in check. His kick was lethal. The mule was danger from start to finish.

Even if television and the movies have slighted the muleskinner, he still maintained more than his share of pride about his vocation. When a veteran muleskinner read in the Bible that it took Moses forty years to lead his people out of Egypt to the Promised Land, he scratched his head and said: "Shucks! Ben Holliday could have fetched them in forty hours."

Muleskinner was not the only appellation for this hero. He was also called muleteer, muledriver, teamster, hair-pounder. These might be the more positive names. The other names should be omitted here. Individually, their names could be anything. Some were nicknamed; some were known by their Christian names; others by surnames. It just happened that way. One was Mr. Church, always with the Mr., if one valued staying alive. There was "Buffalo Jim," the twins, "Curly Dan" and "Curly Jerry" Robbins, Uncle Jim Miller, One-Eyed Charlie, Dutch John and Old Shalcross. (Knights of the Lash).

The muleskinner was a hybrid, maybe like the mule itself, and as much of an enigma. Many observers noted the interacting influences of the mule and the teamster. Many descriptions of the teamsters likened them to drift-wood flotsam in the backwash of the stream of civilization. Many were wanderers, adventurers, romantics and some just out of luck. But a great many were eastern boys who became tired of their lot on the family farm and went West to make a fortune and seek adventure. Almost everyone who went broke turned to the job of driving or teamstering. Many had experienced more noble walks of life. Ex-store keepers, school teachers, doctors and lawyers were sprinkled in the occupation. Probably all of the professions were at one time or another represented, including the clergy. At least one teamster was called "Parson" by his teammates, and, according to observers, displayed all of the traits associated with the profession. One wonders, however, how he could drive his mules without using the only language they understood.

The composite profile of the muleskinner, Anglo-Saxon variety, was by Army General James T. Rusling. He portrayed them as "...outre, red-shirted, big-booted, brigand-looking, ruffians, with their inseparable bowie knife and revolver around their waist, they swung and cracked their great whips like fiends...." A *Harper's* reporter pictured the muleskinner as "sturdy, well-built, tanned by the sun and wind of the plains, hirsuit and unclean in appearance, indicating a 'cat-like" aversion to water." He was more profane than his Mississippi River mate, and, by his own word, "Kin drink more whiskey." He could also be described as vigorous, rollicking, devil-may-care—all of which made him a handsome specimen of western manhood. He invariably had a gorgeous beard and distinguished mustache. Some observers noted that he made fine company if one could put up with some hard profanity. A British reporter noticed that the conversation of some muleskinners was above expectation. Nearly all were literate and "all discussed local and national politics with a terseness and emphasis that would do credit to a professional politician."

The hiring process and interview could be revealing as to the type of person desired. One company official recalled the following interview:

Are you a good driver?
None better!
Did you ever have any accidents?
No Sir!
Did you ever upset a stage or wagon?
No Sir!
Were you ever held up?
No Sir!
Were you ever attacked by Indians?
No Sir!
I am sorry young man, I have no place for you.

Either the young man was lying about having been a driver or had none of the experiences which would make him useful.

Another official recalled this type of interview by a seasoned proprietor who would know the right type when he saw it:

Can you drive?
Yes.
Can you drive like hell?
Yes.
Do you like to work?
The proper answer was "Yes."
Do you drink whiskey?
No. (At this point he probably lied a little.)
You're engaged.
(Knights of the Lash)

W.Z. Hickman related that while each wagon train had a certain core crew of veteran freighters there were many novices and greenhorns on every trip. He noted on one occasion, loading out of Ft. Leavenworth for Denver, the teamsters were hired as they applied without any required references or proven qualifications. Out of the 26 teamsters hired, only 7 had had driving experience and as the writer put it: "they knew as little about driving as a politician knows about honesty." Oftentimes, the first morning out, the wagon-master discovered a number had taken French leave.

The new muleskinner generally arrived on the job without an extra shirt on his back. The first thing that was necessary was to outfit himself for the journey by charging the purchase of rough clothes and boots against his wages. Sometimes, he was required to buy his blankets and a revolver. These purshases meant the teamster had an investment of $40 to $50 before the trip started. His pay was meager, a dollar a day in the early part of the nineteenth century. After the Civil War, the wage had gone up to about $100 a month.

The "Wagon Boss" had to be the best muleskinner on the wagon train. He had to be the most skilled at loading and unloading, the toughest, the quickest draw, the meanest, the best knot maker, the most skilled with the whip, the most creative in obscenity, and the best handler of mules. He also had to be a blacksmith and wheelright to repair a wagon with simple tools. He had to be a hunter to bring in fresh food to enrich what otherwise would be a drab menu. They had to be able to shoe the mules, horses and oxen. He was also expected to be a physician to his men and a veterinarian to his animals. Consequently, one readily can see how valuable a good "wagon boss" was to a successful trip.

Mule driving in the West was something quite different from team driving in the East where the six-mule team was seldom used. For one thing, the reins for each individual team were discarded in favor of a singly line running from the muleskinner to the guide or left, front mule. This mule was called the line mule and the line which connected him to the muleskinner was the only telegraph to transmit messages. Jerking the line caused the lead mule to turn right. A constant and continuous pull guided the lead mule left. The device that conveyed the signal to the rest of the team was a "jockey stick." This item was a short stick, like a broom stick, fastened by a chain to the collar of the guide mule and running to the bit of his companion, the right lead mule. With many turns to be made, this ingenious device would often wear through the skin and reveal raw flesh. Some observers had concluded that the name of "muleskinner" resulted.

The swing team followed the lead team, and then the third team, or wheelers. They were usually the heaviest and strongest team available. They were mainly responsible for getting the wagon started, especially out of a mudhole or ravine or up a steep grade. They also bore the brunt of holding a wagon back when descending, which often could be extremely strenuous and dangerous. The muleskinner rode on the left wheeler, held the guide line in his left hand and his blacksnake whip in his right hand. Often this whip was draped around his neck ready for action, and his right arm poised for immediate use. The two front or lead mules were usually the most spirited animals. The swing team had the easiest assignment. In an eight or ten team wagon, there would be two or three swing teams in the middle between the leaders and wheelers.

Drivers took great pain in decorating their mules. Many would fasten a fox or coyote tail to the bridles and the styles exhibited in the dressing of a mule's tail was enough to make a Paris hairdresser envious. The tails were shaved some distance and then a tuft or bushy ring was left on the tail. This was done two or three times and marked real "mule-dude-ism." Another source of pride for the driver was the mule's coat. Somehow the mule was overendowed by nature with a fine, glossy coat and drivers spent extra hours getting the right shine or sheen.

Without a doubt, the mule that bore the brunt of the duty and the vindictiveness of the muleskinner was the off-wheeler or right side wheel mule. For one thing, he was so close that he could readily be hit or kicked or whipped. When descending a hill, the signal was first given to the off-wheeler by a cut of the whip to start breaking the speed of the wagon.

While teamsters were promiscuous in their profanity, they were selective in the times to use it. On the downhill drive, the teamster generally limited himself to a single word "wah-oo," with the accent on the last syllable. A simple "whoa" was unheard of because that was horse language and mules were thought to ignore it. It was only when the mules became mired in a mud hole or the wheels got caught in some roadside entanglement that the muleskinner opened his rich thesaurus.

All of the above elaborately set the scene for the muleskinner's two most sophisticated talents, cursing and whipping. It was interesting to see the transformation that came over a muleskinner when he was unable to use the full force of his vocabulary to move the mules. This situation generally occurred when a woman or women were nearby. In this uncomfortable circumstance, the driver, obviously vexed and chagrined, did his best by shouting out "What are you doin there Bess? What are you about, Jane? Hey, you, Herman, git to it!" The driver clearly had no faith in this kind of tongue-lashing and he knew that mules didn't either.

The good muleskinner had a voice that thundered. Some said it was like the war cry of a Commanche. William Hooker could hear the expletives a mile away or more. The expert driver had a choice of words that was simply exquistite. His profanity was terrible and unmatched. He had a collection of compound adjectives that equalled anything ever heard.

Standing on his saddle, he vented his whip on the swing mules and the odd-wheeler and dug his heels into the ribs of his saddle mule. His exhortations "baffled all decent description." No one has heard or understood the full eloquence of word power until one has heard a muleskinner discourse with his mules.

Clarence King mountaineering in the Sierra Nevada range told the story of a 12 mule team pulling a wagon loaded high with freight in the mountains. The mules were covered with a white foam of sweat and were breathing like bellows. They clearly were fatigued, completely worn out. The driver knew their condition as he studied the miry spot in which they were stuck. A procession of wagons stretched behind him which intensified the crisis. Cracking his blacksnake whip, the driver tried to pacify the mules by speaking softly to them, hoping that in an unexcited way they could find the courage to strain through this predicament. The mules pulled, lurched, struggled, but to no success. The driver got down and walked alongside the hitch, slashing his whip. The mules tried to respond but ended up in an immovable mound of mule flesh.

Some five wagons behind this disaster was a seasoned muleskinner known as a Pike. Pikes were individuals who came out of the Missouri country, probably Pike County, and were sprinkled about the West. Some said it was a derogatory term which connoted that these individuals had been "puked up" somehow. Regardless, the Pikers knew mules. This one was dressed in a typical costume, a checkered shirt and trousers tucked into his boot tops. He wore a soft, felt hat and it was perched casually on the back of his head and, from underneath the hat, peeked locks of golden hair which hung like a Moslem veil around his florid face. Also visible were sharp, little blue eyes and a long nose.

The Pike observed the tragedy and disaster as long as he could stand it. Then he walked past the intervening wagons with a look of wrath and devilish impatience. Observers expected him to explode with rage, yet his manner seemed controlled. He walked up to the disconcerted driver and gently said, "May I help you?" The muleskinner was only too willing to surrender responsibility for this calamity. The Piker took over. He walked to the lead team and patted them affectionately and pointed them in the right direction. He went back and examined the wagon wheels. Seeing that they were all intact, the Piker began to utter a litany of profanity which began on a

113

fairly low but audible level and continued to grow louder and louder and more and more profane until it erupted in a crescendo of horrid blasphemy. As one observer said, the cursing was so heated and fiendish that one thought that hell had engulfed the earth.

The mules took note and began to respond, except for one laggard, who refused to pull. The Piker went back to this lazy, lop-eared mule, coupled his hands over his mouth and poured into her ear one gigantic oath. The mule sprang forward as if she had been sprung from a bear trap, and, in terror, she lunged against her collar and the traces grated under her strain. By now, all the mules were straining to the fullest. The Piker softly said, in everyday language,

"Come up there mules!" With one quick rumble, the wagon rolled out of the mud hole and was on its way.

The rejoicing teamstser invited the Piker to some liquid refreshments. After the first swallow, the muleskinner turned to the Piker and said, "Well, Billy, you can swear."

"Swear," said the Piker increduously, "Me, swear?" "No, I can't blaspheme worth a cuss. You'd jest orter hear Pete Green. He can exhort the impenitent mule. I've known a ten-mule team to renounce the flesh and haul 31 thousand pounds through a foot of clay mud under one of his outpourings."

Alexander Majors, one of the top executives of the famous shipping firm, Russell, Majors, and Waddell, found religion and began a full campaign against cursing and drinking and fighting among his teamsters. When he hired a teamster, he set down clear rules of behavior and topped it off by presenting the driver with a Bible and a hymn book. One teamster reported that Majors paid him $10 for refraining from profanity during a round trip from Missouri to Santa Fe. There was a song which ridiculed Alexander Major's anti-swearing policy:

You have an awkward team and
A very heavy load.
You have to whip and holler, but
Swear upon the sly.

Rivaling the cursing, the whip was a mean insignia of authority. The length of the whip varied considerably from 8 to 20 feet. It consisted of braided rawhide attached to a 3 or 4 foot stick of hickory. The crack of the whip and the profanity were usually the only prods necessary to move the teams. Obviously, it took experience to master the techniques. A novice easily could entangle his neck in the leather. Contests abounded in the accuracy with which a muleskinner could use his whip. One such contest involved placing a coin on top of a stake driven into the ground. The contestant had to whip the coin off the stake at the predetermined distance without touching the stake. A Harper Magazine reporter told of a bet for a pint of whiskey between two muleskinners. One of them contended that if his friend would bend over he could cut the seat out of his pants without disturbing what was underneath. After all the bets were placed by the contestants and a considerable crowd of spectators, the climatic test of skill occurred. And both contestants lost. One could doubt if the pint of whiskey provided much enjoyment or deadened the pain of the lashing.

One of the most frequently repeated stories of a hair-raising ride involved Horace Greeley. While Mr. Greeley was traveling in the Far West, he had a speaking engagement which could not be missed. He knew the schedule would be tight and so he asked the driver to make every effort to arrive on time. The driver was Hank Monk, one of the most renowned drivers in western history.

Monk gave Greeley a ride which scared the editor beyond anything he could imagine. He begged Monk to forget the schedule; the speech wasn't that important after all. But Monk had made a commitment which had to be fulfilled. With each telling, the story grew and grew. Whenever one met a stranger, one could be sure that sooner or later he would ask about the famous ride of Horace Greeley.

There can be no question that the muleskinners were an exceptional group of people. Most of them had a strong feeling of pride in their accomplishments and their status in the western hierarchy. They were a tough and surly lot who had "...seen the elephant" many times. They were often feared as mean and dangerous people.

Chapter Eleven

Mule vs, Horse

Question: What can a horse do that a mule can't?
Answer: Nothing good.

"A Horse is only half a Mule." Missouri proverb.

The argument has been long and sometimes vitriolic down through the centuries with great ingenuity displayed on both sides. Generally, the horse advocates wouldn't even argue. They usually gave a semblance of a snort which indicated clearly that the answer was so obvious that it did not require an argument. One only had to look at the animals to see the superiority of the horse.

Being more openminded and willing to look at the evidence, the mule advocates were well aware of the fact that one's vision was not always as objective as one would like. What one saw was often colored by what one thought. For the American audience, the mule defenders began their case by quoting George Washington, the father of our country and the man reputed never to have told a falsehood. "For the information of those who are not acquainted with mules, it may be enough to add that their great strength, longevity, hardiness, and cheap support give them a preference to horses that is scarcely imagined," so said our esteemed first president.

One would think that such testimony would be adequate to settle the argument but it is clear that presidents and their judgments have been maligned grossly from the very beginning. Consequently, further evidence had to be presented on behalf of the mule. Of course, such evidence was plentiful.

In early times, the Greeks and Romans had a lofty regard for the mule. The funeral train of Alexander the Great was pulled by 64 mules because the mule's easy and unhurried gait was so gentle that it made an excellent dray for carriage or hearse. Mules pulled chariots at the early Olympic games and many of the imperial Caesars rode in mule powered vehicles. It is said that Nero's mules had their hooves shod with gold and silver. The shoes were not the partial plates with which we are familiar today; these shoes were full plates of gold encircling the entire hoof. Up to the 15th century, French nobles rode large black mules and, during the Renaissance, Cardinals of the Church rode in carriages drawn by handsome white mules.

In early Judea, horses were shunned partly because the Jewish leaders thought that the absence of the horse would protect their isolation and prevent the Jewish people from becoming militaristic and expansionist. Consequently, Saul ordered that no horses were to be taken as booty. David went even further by ordering the horses captured in battle should be killed.

In the early centuries of Christendom, the mule and ass had a place of honor. They had carried the Holy Family and Jesus had chosen the ass for His triumphal entry into Jerusalem. Gradually the image became mixed, sometimes exalted, sometimes ridiculed. By the time of the Middle Ages, a rather elaborate liturgy developed around the ass, but it became a debauchery of an extreme type which showed some of serious problems within Catholicism. The reformers, especially the Calvinists, used the ass to exemplify the wrongs and abuses within the Roman Church and it proved to be a powerful symbol.

This dualism of praise and ridicule has received considerable attention. Scholars and writers have tried to explain it. Robert Graves, the British poet, offered two explanations. First he suggested that the ass had become associated with the Egyptian god, Set, who was known for his cruelty and wickedness. The anger and ridicule directed against Set, also was directed against the ass. This happened early on and continued through the years. Graves's second explanation was derived from the Middle Ages and the winter Saturnalia festival at which an ass-like god with long-ears was killed by his rival. Graves said this yearly event developed into the tradition in which a Christmas fool wore an ass-eared cap and was killed by the spirit of the new year. Frederick Zeuner argued that the mule developed a low social status because its meekness and patience gave it the characteristics of a slave. In most countries, the ass or mule became the poor man's "horse."

The reputation of the horse went in the opposite direction. He became associated with the knights and military exploits and thus was associated with power, glory and pride of accomplishment.

Consequently, the tide of history has not been kind to the mule or ass. However, in democratic America they were given a chance to redeem themselves. Social mobility or fluidity was extolled. Prestige and honor were not bestowed on one by birth; they had to be won by deed and action. Especially on the frontier, one had to prove oneself by action. If one pretended importance, affluence or superiority in the West, he could be sure that he would be challenged quickly, most often to a fight of some kind.

The mule took advantage of this Land of Opportunity to re-establish its honor and good name. Many farmers and westerners regarded the mule more highly than the horse. In practical terms, the mule was an easier keeper. He ate less than a horse, lived longer, and could work harder for more hours per day and for more years. Under difficult circumstances, the mule would outlive a horse by about four years. Under light circumstances, the mule would outlive the horse by a much greater number of years.

The American Farmer also pointed out that, in summer, the mule can subsist on grass alone, and in winter, when not worked, can feed on hay without decline of health. The horse must be supplied some grain the whole year. If fed corn, the mule will eat 4 to 8 ears a day, while the horse will eat twice as much. Very importantly, the mule knows when to quit eating. He will only eat as much as he needs and then walk away. The horse will continue to eat as long as there is food. Consequently he can overeat and founder.

The advantages of the mule's self-discipline and control of his appetite might not be evident to some observers. W.B. Rose of Richmond, Missouri explained it in very clear terms:

"We used to put the mules in a pen, feed 'em in a trough. We didn't feed 'em but twice a week. Just fill the trough plumb full. Get up of a morning and you go up to the barn to get some mules, why all you've gotta do is put the bridles on 'em and the harness on 'em. They've already had their breakfast. They've been eatin' as they need to. And a horse, you cain't do 'em thataway. You've gotta hand-feed 'em."

Not only is the mule easier to feed, he will eat almost anything. Some farmers said that they had the appetite of a termite. It defied description, rationality or explanation. In desperate situations, mules would eat almost anything including their teammate's tail. During the Civil War, a team of mules actually ate a government wagon. On another occasion, a starved mule ate a soldier's overcoat.

Another positive point for the mule that farmers prized was the mule's sociability. If a moderate number of horses, especially stallions, were placed in the same pen, it wouldn't be long before they would be fighting for precedence and leadership. Mules, on the other hand, would endure one another in a much more friendly and accepting manner. The advantage of this virtue from the farmer's point of view was that he could place mules in a pen very inexpensively. Horses would have to be put into stalls so they couldn't get at one another.

In addition, the mule must be shod only once a year, while a horse will require shoeing four times. This factor, along with the smaller feed bill, made the mule a much cheaper animal to use.

The distinguished Southern journalist, Ralph McGill, argued that the mule combined the best features of his parents. It had the wit, sobriety, endurance and sure-footedness of the Jack; the strength and bulk of the horse. It thrived on poor food and withstood cold or blistering heat.

Longevity and hardiness were big factors on the frontier. The *St. Louis Missouri Democrat* reported that it had numerous accounts of mules attaining the age of forty, fifty and sixty years. Colonel Middleton of South Carolina reported that he had one who reached 80. The paper reported that there was a mule in Ireland who had lived 151 years. Although this was highly uncommon, mules often lived to 40 and this factor added much to their value.

In many ways the mule was smarter and more talented than the horse. If a barn caught on fire, which they often did back in the old days, a horse would panic, freeze in his place and die in the fire. The mule would keep his senses and try to find a way to escape, which he often did. Mules were known to have jumped down to the ground from considerable heights to save themselves from a fire.

If a mule got caught in a fence, particularly a barbed wire fence, he would freeze until someone came to set him free. A horse, in a similar situation, would trash about and try to free himself. Some were known to saw off a foot by rubbing and kicking against the wire. They often did themselves serious injury.

Both mules and horses were prone to runaway. However, the horse did it in a frenzy, often running headlong into objects such as trees or walls, or into ditches. In other words, they usually hurt themselves seriously when they ran away. The mule did it with a more controlled frenzy; he avoided obstacles and hurting himself. Usually, after some distance, the mule would stop and gather himself together.

J. Frank Doby related his experience with a team of mules called

Maggy and Tol. Although he had taken many airplane rides, the fastest thing he ever rode was an empty wagon pulled by Maggy and Tol. They avoided every tree, didn't run into a fence, but their full mulespeed over trails, bushes and prickley pear clumps gave Doby an excitement unduplicated by any other experience.

After the Civil War, many veterans recalled that they saw many more dead horses than dead mules during the war. Tex Ewell checked Western journals of the pioneers and he found 20 dead horses alongside the road for every dead mule. Mark Twain pointed out in his book, Roughing It, that mules replaced horses in the "difficult country." John Anderson Miller wrote an interesting book about the use of street cars in the big cities. He concluded that the companies preferred mules to horses to pull the street cars because two mules could be fed for the cost of one horse and the mules could do one-third more work. They could also stand the summer heat better. In St. Louis, the one-mule streetcars were called "dinkies" or "jackrabbit cars."

Clarence Cannon, once a powerful representative from Missouri in the U.S. Congress, said that the Missouri Mule was the most indestructible agricultural implement ever devised.

Most farmers ended up admitting that the mule outsmarted them on most occasions. Henry Graddy, a longtime mule breeder in Kentucky, was convinced that mules could reason. "If you impose on one, he'll resent it." Graddy sold jacks to Nelson Rockefeller of New York for his ranch in Venezuela.

Melvin Bradley, a retired professor of animal husbandry, after many conversations with farmers and livestock dealers and handlers, reported that these people generally spoke with much more affection and higher esteem for their mules than for their horses. They recalled stories more readily about their mules and they could remember more often the names of their mules.

There is an old Texas saying:
"Give me a mule and a plow,
And a cow and a sow,
And I'll get along somehow."

In Texas also, there is a town called Muleshoe, and in the center of this town, is a big statue to honor the mule. A number of years ago, some citizens wanted to rename the town from Muleshoe to Rosebud. The projected change aroused such a furor from the oldtimers that the name remained Muleshoe. It is more than fitting that the oldtimers won. After all, Kansas City has perched on a tall pedestal over the stockyards on the western edge of the downtown area a statue of a Hereford bull. In Sumner, Missouri, "Maxie," a 61 foot statue of a Canadian Goose poised for flight, pays homage to the 200,000 geese which annually visit the "Goose Capitol of the world.

In Warrensburg, Missouri, a life-sized replica of "Old Drum", a hound dog, keeps a vigil at the courthouse where Senator George Graham gave his memorable eulogy to the dog, man's "one absolutely unselfish friend." Not to belittle the wondrous quality of a dog, but Warrensburg really should have a statue for the mule. The city prizes an old Mule Barn and the athletic teams of the local Central Missouri State University are known as the MULES. Warrensburg was a large mule producing and trading center in the Mule Era.

For Louis Monsees, the famous Missouri jack breeder, the question of superiority between mule and horse was an easy question to answer. Mr. Monsees had acquired in his many trades an outlaw mule which he called Peggy. Peggy was a shiney, jet black, with a mealy nose. She was downright mean and many thought untameable. She was especially known for her ferocious bucking.

Louis Monsees personally took charge of her reeducation and he completely changed her personality. It is not known if he used facets of the Skinnerian method of behavior modification. Whatever form the treatment took, Peggy became not only a great saddle mule but also a family pet.

Peggy did not lose one bit of her intelligence in the process of domestication. She could open latches, tie or untie a knot, open and close doors, and remove her harness. Peggy contributed to the belief that a mule could take a "pin and pick a padlock" by opening every barn door and helping herself to the corn and oats. Special safeguards had to be taken to prevent Peggy's marauding.

Peggy was dependable, however, and Louis Monsees came to trust her completely. It was the day before the common use of the telephone and telegraph. Buyers of jacks and jennies would come to the Limestone Valley Farm without advance notice. Louis began to use Peggy to take the buyers from the farm back to Smithton to catch the late evening train.

When the stockmen arrived at the railway depot, they were instructed to throw the reins over the buckboard and Peggy would make her way home under her own power and guidance. So successful did

121

this system become that Monsees began to send Peggy into town to meet the trains. Customers would arrive at the station and ask the ticket agent how to get to the Limestone Valley Farm. The agent would point to Peggy and say: "Just get in the buggy and you're practically there."

Going up to the farm, Peggy approached the long swinging gate, manuevered the buggy until she could nudge the wooden latch. When the gate swung open, Peggy would push her way through. The gate was set on a slight incline, and as soon as the rear wheels had passed through, the gate would swing back and lock itself. Peggy would let the visitors off at their proper lodgings. The bewildered guests wondered what amount to tip such a resourceful and thoughtful servant.

In the mountains and canyons, there is no question of the mule's superiority in trail riding and packing. Many miners and fortune seekers developed strong attachments to their mules and burros. They were more sure-footed, and had a tougher hide so that they could endure more severe weather and could carry rougher and heavier loads.

Buffalo Bill Cody told an interesting story in his autobiography about the superiority of his mule over General George Custer's horse. In the winter of 1866-67, Cody met Custer when Custer needed a guide to take him to Fort Larned, a distance of 65 miles from where they were. Custer was in a hurry, as usual, and he was somewhat upset that Cody was riding a mule because the mule would be too slow.

Cody assured the general that the mule was better than any horse around. They started out riding side by side. Cody said that his mule had such a fast walk that Custer's horse, a fine Kentucky thoroughbred, had to half-trot to keep up.

Whenever Custer wasn't looking, Cody slyly spurred the mule ahead, and when he started forward, Cody would feign reining him in and bidding him not to be too fractious. In this way, Cody set a lively pace all morning long. After 25 miles, they stopped to rest the animals. After only a short stop, Custer was anxious to start again. Cody advised an easier gait since they still had 40 miles to go. But Custer wanted a faster pace. Cody continued the same tactics he had used earlier. He pretended to be checking his mule while he was really pushing him to a rather fast pace.

Presently, they noticed that the escorting party was lagging far behind. Custer observed that they were setting too fast a pace for the other horses. Cody replied that this was the usual pace for his mule and he supposed that Custer was in a hurry. Several times they had to stop and wait for the other soldiers to catch up. Their horses were panting and sweating, and were reaching the limit of their endurance.

When they reached a high ridge overlooking the Pawnee Fork, they again had to wait for the others. As they waited, Cody said to Custer: "If you want to send a dispatch ahead to the officer in command at Fort Larned, I will be pleased to take it down for you. You can follow this ridge till you come to the creek and then follow the valley right down to the fort."

When the group caught up with them, Custer turned to the Captain and repeated to him Cody's instructions on how to reach the Fort. Custer then turned to Cody: "I shall ride ahead with you. Now, Cody, I am ready for you and that mouse-colored mule."

They took off and Cody recorded that from then on they were "some going." When they got to the fort, Custer dismounted and turned his horse over to an orderly for care. Cody personally cared for his mule to make sure he would be ready the next morning. The next day, bright and early, Cody had breakfast, groomed and saddled his mule and rode to the general's quarters. When Custer appeared, Cody saluted and said he was ready to go.

"I am not feeling very pleasant this morning, Cody, my horse died during the night." Cody said that he was sorry that the general's horse got into too fast a class the day before.

"Well," Custer replied, "hereafter I will have nothing to say against a mule. We will meet again on the Plains. I shall try to have you detailed as my guide, and then we will have time to talk over that race."

Some people argued that a mule was smarter than a dog, and since the dog was smarter than a horse, it figured that a mule was smarter than a horse too. So the story about Joe Kendig, the Pennsylvania Dutch trader, and his mule, Mistress Mollie, is very fitting. Mollie was a family pet. Kendig had bought her in Missouri to be resold in Pennsylvania. But the mule was so intelligent and lovable, that the family decided to keep her. Everyone liked Mistress Molly, except one of the dogs. Every evening when Mollie trotted out of the barn for a drink of water, the dog would be there to bark and snap at her heels. The mule would run a short distance, turn quickly, and kick at the dog. But the dog was smart, he knew exactly how close he could get. He had every step marked and measured. Every evening the ritual was the same. Neither protagonist changed the strategy.

And so it went until one summer evening. There had been a sudden summer rain which left the ground slippery. Mollie emerged from the barn on schedule and the dog darted for her heels barking. Mollie whirled, but then the story changed.

The dog had his paces counted, but he slipped. This time the mule's feet caught him dead-center. He went flying through the air, yelping as he flew. Mollie turned to pursue the dog and put an end to him once and for all time.

When the dog landed, he immediately made for the barn to find a safe hiding place. Mollie undertook a thorough examination of the barn to find her tormentor. Every stall, feed trough, bale of hay or straw, every nook and cranny was carefully examined. Finally Mollie gave up the search and went out into the yard for her drink. About a hour later, the dog crawled out of a feed barrel and stole away. But Mollie had won her contest. Never again did the dog snap or bark when she went trotting by.

Pat Talburt of Branson, Missouri, had an unusual argument to prove the mule's superiority over the horse in intelligence. Pat put it this way: "A mule seems to be about twice as smart as a horse, to our way of thinking, anyway. We can potty-train a mule. Be drivin' a wagon around the park, the mule's tail comes up and ole Tom Ristead, the guy drivin', says: 'Ahhh, get that tail down.' They put the tail down. They wait 'til he takes 'em off the park to go to the bathroom. A horse will just go anywhere at any time, while he's walkin', while he's runnin', doesn't matter. There's a.....a mule is kind of mysterious. a mysterious type animal."

Carl Russell said that mules "...mind better. There's something about a mule. If he ever gets a good habit, he never forgets it. And when you're breakin' 'em, you have to be careful and not let 'em get the bad habits. And they'll always love you for it!"

Many successful mule farmers, like Booker T. Van of Portageville, Missouri, stressed talkin' to your mules to make 'em behave and work hard. Van thought the mule was smarter than a horse because "...you could talk to that mule. You don't have to whup him. You talk to him and he'll do just what you tell him to do....You talk to him, especially on a rainy day. I used to slip in the kitchen, steal my momma's sugar, and give 'em a little sugar once in awhile. They'll eat sugar outta your hand. You don't need no 2 X 4, no sir."

The final clinching argument for the mule's superiority came from Cornell University where a group of scientists undertook an experiment to test animal intelligence. Their tests revealed that the horse was quite low in grey matter, only slightly higher than a sheep and about on the same level as a cow. The mule proved smarter on all the tests given. Of course, the horse lovers argued that the tests were poorly designed, that they were culturally biased by not including real live horse experiences. Who is able to define "intelligence" anyway? And, even if it could be defined satisfactorily, who could possibly measure it with any accuracy and reliability?

And so the argument continues into the next millennium. However, the mule people know the right answer.

Chapter Twelve

The Military Mule

A raw recruit is inducted into the Army with a burr haircut and a set of dog tags. The mule recruit was inducted with his dog tags burned or branded into his hide. An inexperienced observer might think that the brand "U S" stood for the United States or Uncle Sam. The veterans knew better. It stood for Un Safe.

The most common Army name for the mule in World War II was "Jughead." However one sergeant called his mule "Circumstance." When asked why, the sarge replied: Haven't you ever had a circumstance over which you had no control?

The Army mule probably felt like "GI Joe." Along with everything else, he was "government issue." Nothing fit and everything usually was messed up thoroughly. Hurry up and wait in endless lines. Orders and more orders, often contradictory. Bill Mauldin often used mules in his World War II cartoons. One of these cartoons showed a mule delivering a Lieutenant to the troops on the front line. When Willie saw the officer, he angrily said: "Dammit, ya promised to bring rations this trip."

Despite the errors and unplanned chaos, the mule served his country with distinction in all the wars through the Korean conflict. Vietnam was the first war in which the American Army chose not to enlist the mule's services. The results were a debacle of the highest order. In the minds of many military analysts, the defeat and the failure to use mules were directly and intimately connected as cause and effect. It is difficult to understand how the Joint Chiefs could have made such an egregious mistake.

For many years of the country's history, the government has been the largest mule owner in the world. James W. Stoole was of the opinion that "...the two matters of greatest importance in military affairs are, first, the health and efficiency of the men; and second, the condition of the mules.

The American war in which the mule played its largest role was the Civil War. The North and the South enlisted over 600,000 mules, about evenly divided. They were utilized as pack carriers and wagon pullers for supplies and artillery. Although both sides started with roughly equal numbers, the South soon became disconnected from the supply sources. Yankee strategy focused on this goal early in the war because the Northerners recognized how important transport would be since they had industrial superiority over the South. The Northern armies soon occupied all the main areas wherein mules were manufactured thus the South was unable to recruit new animals to replace her casualties.

At least on one occasion, the mules won single-handedly a signficant battle for the Northern army. During the Chattanooga campaign, both armies, probing for the right place and the right time to launch a major attack, made contact at the wrong place and at the wrong time. The two armies met at Wauhatchie, Tennessee, October 28, 1863, in one of the rare night battles of the war.

At the climax of the engagement between General Longstreet's Confederate Forces and General Geary's Federal Troops, a group of Hooker's Yankee teamsters became so terrified that they deserted their charges. The muleskinners' fears were transmitted to the mules and they broke loose and ran in a wild stampede. Fortunately for the Northern Army, the mules ran pellmell into a pocket of the Confederate Infantry.

Thinking the noise and din from the charging steeds could only mean a cavalry attack, the Confederate troops withdrew. Grant concluded that the Confederates "...took this (stampeding mules) for a charge and stampeded in turn." It was clearly a mule victory and everyone, including the Army brass, realized it.

Then the problem arose of how to devise a fitting reward and recognition for the mules. The Army thought and thought. The officers concluded that the highest recognition which they could bestow upon the mules for their great courage under fire and for their service above and beyond the call of duty would be to grant them the "brevet rank of horse." This award of "brevet" meant that the promotion to a higher rank was without a raise in pay. On top of that, what mule would regard being called a "horse" a promotion or an honor?

On one occasion, President Lincoln was informed that the enemy had captured a general and forty mules. After some reflection, Lincoln lamented: "I sure hate to lose those forty mules." The president understood clearly how important the mules were in supplying the army. With that knowledge, Lincoln could endure hearing a Confederate taunt:

"Jefferson Davis rode a dapple gray, Lincoln rode a mule, Jefferson Davis is a gentleman, and Lincoln is a fool."

With only a few exceptions, the mule avoided cavalry duty and left that dubious honor mostly to the horse. Clearly this was how the mule wanted it. Observers noted that mules hated the drilling and the marching back and forth. They thought it was sheer nonsense and a waste of effort to be wheeling about the drill field, doing fours right and left, back and forth, over and over. More importantly, they were farsighted enough to see that cavalry duty led to reckless cavalry charges into the enemy's line. The mule understood why the mortality rate was so much higher for the horse.

A few generals on each side preferred to ride mules rather than horses despite the Army caste system. General Sterling Price, in Missouri, rode a mule into battle. When Price died, a monument was planned in his honor. Some suggested that a statue be made with the General astride a Missouri mule. But the idea was vetoed because the critics thought it would be undignified. The mule was eliminated and the General stood alone.

General Jo Shelby's mule fared somewhat better. Minstrels composed a special song to honor "Shelby's Mule."

> "'Tis true he had to succomb and others now hold rule
> Yet the boys all say they'll pack the State down South
> on Shelby's mule."

Anyone who has studied the Civil War in Missouri is thoroughly acquainted with this famous mule.

On another front, the mule provided much of the humor in maintaining the morale of the troops on both sides. The mule's greatest contribution may have been his talent for diversion. He broke the monotony of Army life and relieved the anxiety amidst all the carnage. The mule looked funny and acted funnier. It did not matter how simple a mule story might be; it was still humorous. One of General Lee's mule companies called itself: "Lee's Miserables," after Victor Hugo's novel, Les Miserables. After the war, the North awarded disability pensions to over a thousand soldiers for their injuries from being too close to mules.

On one occasion, Union troops were shut up in and around Chattanooga before the battle of Lookout Mountain. They could not get relief and they were suffering from hunger. One soldier testified that this starvation had gone on for three months. His outfit had three crackers a day, what corn they could steal from the starving mules, and some half-ripe persimmons.

One day a mule had gotten stuck in the mud and had injured itself so badly that it had to be killed. Very quickly, 200 men surrounded the carcass, and, within minutes, only the hoofs were left. Two members of the "Hundred and Dutch" Regiment hotly contested rights to the tail. While they fought, someone stole the tail, leaving the two combatants only black eyes and bloody noses.

In a similar situation near Vicksburg, some starving Confederates composed a menu to make light of their suffering. It included just about everything they could imagine with the mule being the main ingredient. Some of the choices were Mule Tail Soup, Mule Bacon, Mule Ham, Mule Sirloin, Mule Head Stuffed A-La-Mode, Mule Ears Fricassed A-La-Gotch, Mule Spare Ribs, Mule Liver Hashed, Mule Salad, Mule Hoof Soused, Mule Brains A-La-Omelette, Mule Kidney Stuffed with Peas, Mule Tripe Fried in Pea Meal Batter, Mule Tongue Cold A-La-Bray.

Another Civil War story focused on "Ole Whitey" who had C.S.A. (Confederate States of America) branded on his hide. Ole Whitey supposedly broke away from a Confederate corral and swam the Rappahannock River to fight Yankee mules in hoof to hoof combat. One Yankee wagonmaster tried to put Ole Whitey to work which was anathema to this particular renegade. He preferred to search the campsites for a good fight.

On one occasion, he almost met his match. He picked a fight with a dun-colored Union mule called "Dynamite" who had a "doubleback action kick with a cylinder attachment and a smokeless explosion." The two mules confronted one another. As if by a signal from an unseen referee, the mules stood on their hind legs, pawed, hammered, and bit each other. Then they turned and stood on their front legs and kicked with full power from their business ends. The dun mule made one mistake; he turned broadside and lowered his guard. Ole Whitey let him have it with both feet and Dynamite fell to the ground. Old Whitey let out a triumphant bray and walked away.

Union troops wondered if Old Whitey was a Trojan mule planted by the Rebs to create havoc and chaos in the Yankee mulestock. Or was he an honest mule who simply liked a good fight?

Although he was no military hero, Mark Twain rode a mule throughout his interesting, but short and ill-fated, career as a Marion Ranger in the Civil War. After a few weeks of service, he fell out of a hayloft and incapacitated himself for the remainder of the conflict. Fighting didn't hold much attraction for him anyway.

Before the accident, a friend loaned Twain a small yellow mule by the name of "Paint Brush." This mule provided much amusement because of his extremely small size and his tendency to buck. Twain seemed to spend as much time trying to remount as he did riding.

Paint Brush had all of the traits of the legendary Missouri mule. He would stand and bray, stretch his neck, lay back his ears and spread his jaws, "until you could see right down to his works," as Twain put it. Once Twain tried to lead him off the drill field but the intractable animal lowered his ears, dug in his hoofs, and refused to budge. But the old river man was equal to the situation. The ex-river boat pilot put a rope on the mule and tied it to a nearby well handle, and "fetched him home with a windlass."

On another day, the mule and Twain were reconnoitering with a fellow soldier, Abe Grimes, who was mounted on a huge horse which made Paint Brush look even smaller than he was. They came to the Missouri River which they needed to cross. Paint Brush refused to enter the water. Abe Grimes tied one end of a long rope around Paint Brush's neck and the other end around the horse's saddle horn. Abe's horse then proceeded to swim across the river, pulling the mule and Twain into the water.

When Grimes got to the other side, he looked back and could not see the mule or his rider. With some panic, he spurred him mule up the bank and out into the adjoining field. Eventually, the two lost souls appeared, soaking wet. After Twain wiped the water out of his eyes and ears, he said to Abe: "Abe, you know what? That darn little devil refused to swim. He insisted on walking across the river on the bottom."

Shortly thereafter, Twain discharged himself from the service and took off for the Far West. Although he never commented on this decision, it undoubtedly removed Twain from ever being considered for the American presidency or vice-presidency.

One military shortcoming of the mule was his inclination to bray at very inopportune times and thus betray to the enemy his force's location. General Stonewall Jackson, the father of modern military mobility, loved to appear suddenly in unexpected places and destroy an enemy force. Jackson was also a prayerful man.

Once General Jackson had to move a large force through enemy lines without being detected. If the mules started braying, as was their want, the manuever would end in disaster. The General consulted his quartermaster, Colonel Mason. The Colonel advised that they tie every mule's tail to his belly. Mason had observed that a mule had to raise his tail before he could bray.

Jackson ordered the instructions to be followed. Then a mare horse led the "muzzled" pack through the forest and enemy lines. Not a single mule brayed. When the assignment was completed, Colonel Mason repeated his unforgettable words to General Jackson: "The mule never brays until he first lifts his tail." Some of the soldiers wondered however if the string around the mule's tail or the General's prayers saved the night by silencing the mules.

During World War I, there was some anecdotal evidence that the Army actually performed some corrective surgery on the mule's tail to control the braying. A Texas Ranger confirmed the anecdotal history that a mule cannot bray unless its tail is in the proper position. A scout for a freighting company recalled that mules were debrayed by cutting a small cord beneath the tail close by the mule's hip. Needless to say, the operation was performed without anesthesia.

After the Civil War, the Army became embroiled in the Indian Wars on the western frontier. One of the true heroes in these struggles was General George Crook. Crook perceived correctly that the Army had to become more mobile if it was to contend with the quick-striking Indian forces. To achieve this mobility, Crook perfected the mule pack train. He studied the whole process with nothing left unexamined.

Meticulous manuals were prepared on how every function could be performed efficiently and quickly. How to pack and unpack. What knots to use and when. What saddles and cradles to use for the various kinds of cargo. What men made the best packers and how tall they had to be. What exercises prepared these men for their tasks. What to feed the animals. When and how much to water. What size of mules to use for the different loads and terrain. Absolutely nothing was overlooked or omitted.

Unlike most military manuals, this one was well received because the men and mules recognized the genius behind it. Most importantly, it provided the needed mobility and gave the Army the upper hand in the West. In the process, Crook advanced the prestige and honor of the mule who played his position like an All-American team member.

To top it all, Crook rode a mule. He was fastidious in his dress, as one might imagine about a person who paid such close attention to details. He wore a magnificent forked beard. He loved to hunt and would often strike a Napoleonic pose with his hand in his blouse and his foot on the fallen prey. Grant recognized Crook's abilities and elevated him early to the rank of General in 1871 when few officers were being promoted to this level.

In addition to the mule's greater prestige and his own personal advancement, Crook made the packer and the mule-skinner into true professionals. He respected them and sharpened their skills to new heights of excellence.

On the other side, General George Armstrong Custer ignored the lessons of General Crook and didn't recognize the critical value of mule pack support. Custer paid the ultimate price for his foolishness and vainglory. He disobeyed Crook's orders, misplayed his hand at several strategic points, and lost the battle at the Little Big Horn. General Crook knew the importance of the pack mule and he also had a more intelligent and humane understanding of the Indian.

During the Spanish-American War in the late 1890s, Mr. Dooley pronounced: "What is needed to carry this war is an 'armer' of jacks and mules. What do you say to a mule? Get-up, whoa, gee, haw, back-up, get-along! He don't know what you're drivin' at or to, but a mule hars the orders with a melancholy smile, droops his ears, and follows his warm moist breath. Th' orders from Washington is perfectly comprehensible to a Jackass, but they don't mean anything to a poor, foolish man."

World War I provided new opportunities for the mule and a return to the Old World of Europe. The British prized the mule's military capability so much that they bought over 300,000 mules and horses from the Guyton and Harrington Company in Lathrop, Missouri. The English soldiers praised their mules—"those bloody creatures so hard-hearted under fire."

Mules also served American forces in France, especially the Artillery units. More than 50,000 mules served in the fighting in France. Harry S Truman achieved his officer status as an Artillery Officer partially because of his farm-learned skills in handling mules and horses. In addition, Truman had learned the effective art of cursing from his mule handling background.

When Truman was confronted by a potential stampede under heavy enemy gunfire, much like the one described above at Chattanooga, Truman stopped the rearward charge with some well chosen expletives. His men and mules froze in their tracks and stood firm for the attack. so inspiring was Truman's language.

In World War II, the mule performed in at least 10 different theatres of war operations. He acted heroically in Burma and Italy where the mountainous areas made the Jeep and other mechanical equipment less effective. One Army General said that the Appenines of Italy seemed to scream out the need for mules if the Allies hoped to win.

Once in Burma, the Army was moving along a narrow mountain trail with disaster only inches away if someone would slip and lose his footing. At one point the trail was too loose and a mule lost his footing and went plummeting down the mountain side a thousand feet or more with a heavy load on his back. No one thought the mule could survive such a punishing fall head over heels over and over again.

After swallowing their anguish over the lost mule, the soldiers continued their march. Three days later, they were brought to an abrupt stop by the sound of braying to the rear. Eventually, what should appear? The "Dead Mule." How did he survive the fall? How did he claw his way up the mountain side to regain the trail? How did he find and catch up with his outfit? Everyone knew it couldn't happen, but, here he was ready to resume his place in the ranks.

World War II brought a new challenge to the mule, the Jeep. Undoubtedly, the jeep was a wonderful invention for the Army. Its versatility and durability were outstanding. GI Joe was extremely creative in his uses for the jeep. Bill Mauldin showed a GI racing a jeep up a hill so he could have hot water to shave. Certainly this was one feature the mule could not match. But both the mule and the jeep were versatile, durable, rugged and, nearly, indestructible. The Jeep had four wheel drive to match the four legged mule. One expert called the jeep a "no nonsense solution to a problem of transportation." The mule was a nonsense solution. One had to be young and limber to ride a jeep, the same was true for mule riding. After the war, it was said that the jeep could be used to plow, harrow or disc, and to do other farm chores—just like a mule.

In the 1950s, the Army considered replacing the jeep with a new vehicle called the "Mutt." It was even closer to the mule in capabilities, and, it had the first two letters right in its name. The Army published a photograph of a young Corporal crying beside his defunct jeep, a casualty of enemy gunfire. The corporal was saying: "You don't understand; I loved this jeep." How many mule men said the same thing beside their dead mule. Once a captured Indian Kiowa Chief, Santanta, pleaded with the Army officers to let him keep his mule: "I have come to love him as a son."

One of the boldest decisions of President Harry Truman concerned the desegregation of the Armed Forces. By Executive Order, Truman demanded the integration of the Armed Forces. The big shortcoming of this order, however, was that it did not go far enough. The Order did not command equal treatment and rights for the mule compared to the horse. The mule continued to suffer discrimination and he was not allowed the rights and privileges accorded the horse.

One of the most flagrant violation of rights involved a mule at Fort Carson, Colorado. The animal's name was "Hambone". He was often entered in jumping events under the alias of "Mr. Hamilton T. Bone." Oftentimes, he won several ribbons in the same show, but would have to return them when the judges found out he was a mule. He really embarrassed the horse set when he won the jumper classic at the Camp Carson Hunt Club. After this humiliation, the Hunt Club refused to let him enter any further competition.

Despite his plebian ancestry, Hambone received such wide publicity over his accomplishments and athletic ability, that *Life* Magazine ran a multi-page story on him in 1949. Two soldiers even wrote a song about him. There was no question that he was the favorite mount for the children at Fort Carson; the horses had no chance against him.

One would think that President Truman, having been called a Missouri Mule himself, would have had the courage to go all the way in his Executive Order on desegregation. Undoubtedly, he would have been charged with "conflict of self-interest" but fairness and justice demanded such courage.

Although the military future looks bleak for the mule, especially after the star-wars weaponry of the Gulf War, one should be extra careful about predicting the end of the military mule. Too many conditions still exist around the world under which the mule can function and other equipment and personnel cannot.

———— Chapter Thirteen ————
Mythology And the Mule

Mythology and greatness are closely linked. Historians and political scientists have established the ability to generate myths as one of the main criterion for determining the greatness of a leader. If this is a valid measure, then surely the mule should have a claim to greatness in history.

The mule's peculiar characteristics and natural proclivities caused many interesting ideas and explanations about his origins and behavior. It was certainly not an error in cosmic architecture that kept the mule out of the Garden of Eden. For equally obvious reasons Noah excluded him from the Ark. Some legends say that the mule refused to walk up the gangway to the Ark. The Book of Genesis did not mention him, nor the Book of Revelation. But he and his ancestral ass are mentioned frequently in the other biblical texts.

Like every illegitimate child, the mule has had a troubled life. He is tainted with the black tar of perversion. His very existence is a biological puzzle. Pre-industrial people invented many myths around the mule. It is one of the most frequently mentioned animals in Aesop's Fables. These fables grew out of Greek life and society and are similar to stories from other early civilizations. Aesop had over 25 fables which involved the donkey. In virtually every case the donkey is depreciated or demeaned.

In one fable the donkey appealed to Zeus for relief from his life of toil with a gardner. Zeus consented and assigned the ass to a potter. The donkey was even more unhappy because he had to carry even heavier loads. He appealed to Zeus a second time. The god consented again to the donkey's request and assigned him to a tanner. After a time, the donkey was more distressed than ever. "If die here, I will not even be buried."

Another time, a donkey heard the locusts singing and he thought their song was simply beyond compare. He wanted to sing as they did. He asked the locusts what they ate that made their voices so beautiful. When they told him that they ate the dew, the donkey went on a dew diet and starved to death.

One Aesop fable allowed the donkey to come out satisfactorily and that story involved Doctor Wolf. Once upon a time, a donkey was apprehended by a wolf. Seeing that there was no escape, the donkey pretended lameness and told the wolf that he had picked up a thorn in his foot. He asked the wolf to remove the thorn so that it would not stick in the wolf's throat when he devoured the donkey. The wolf thought that this request was reasonable. He picked up the donkey's foot to look for the thorn and the donkey let fly with a powerful kick which broke the wolf's jaw and broke off his teeth. The wolf lamented that he probably got what he deserved. Afterall, his father had taught him to be a butcher, why should he want to be a doctor?

In many fables, men are changed into beasts or beasts into men. Sometimes the beast is an ass. The remedy might be the eating of a rose petal. The moral of such fables can be many. One can read into the story that humans may degrade their minds and bodies by sensual and beastly pleasures and thus lose their reason and values. We regain them by renouncing the sensuous life. Another explanation might be that an ignorant man is an ass without wit or wisdom. As he eats of the flower of knowledge, he acquires wisdom and casts off his beastly shape. Or perhaps, it is a story of a youth full of indiscretion who commits many follies. But he finally matures and casts off his youthful ways.

In Lucian''s *Lucius or the Ass*, the theme took yet another turn which is humorous and extolled the ass' capabilities. It seemed that the hero was turned somehow into a lowly ass. He remained in this shape for a very long time. But a beautiful maiden fell in love with the ass. When the hero was restored to his human condition, he returned to the girl who had loved him in his lowly state. She invited him to spend the night. Alas, when he attempted to imitate the donkey in order to regain her affection, she became so disaffected that she screamed: "Go and sleep somewhere else!" "Why, what on earth have I done?" he asked. "Oh, for God's sake, don't you understand?" she exclaimed. "It was the donkey I fell in love with, not you!" The hero was turned out of the house and spent the night in deep remorse.

In Eastern mythology, the ass was not an object of ridicule as often as in the West. Some writers thought the reason to be that the Eastern varieties of the asinine family were more handsome and noble in appearance. In the East, the ass was portrayed generally as ardent, lively, and swiftfooted; whereas the Western ass was slow, lazy, and having no real energy except of a sensual nature.

Consequently, many Western stories focused on the lascivious aspect. After all, so many young lovers became asses over the love of a fair maiden. The ass' milk was prized in many places as the nectar or ambrosia of romance.

Another mythological theme centered on the big ears of the ass or mule. Since they were so large and provided such acute hearing, the ass was often presented as the possessor of secrets. He even knew the devil's secrets since he was so often in the devil's company.

Many kings and princes were cursed with exceptionally large ears because of some wrongdoing or foolishness. So afflicted, the king or prince would impose an oath of secrecy on his attendants so the public would not learn of the deformity. Many servants lost their lives because such a secret was difficult to keep.

On one occasion, a young handsome courtier became seriously ill from trying to keep such a secret. Finally, he just had to tell someone. So he went into a remote field and whispered the secret about the king's ears into a squirrel hole. As most people know, animals can hear, understand, and speak. Eventually, the king learned that the young man had divulged the secret. But, when he discovered how it had happened, the king relented, pardoned him, and even made the young man his prime minister.

As one of his first acts, the new prime minister designed a new hat in the shape of the ears of an ass in order to conceal the king's deformity. The hat was so beautiful and attractive that the king would wear it publicly with pride. The people loved it too and many began to wear similar hats. The king came out of seclusion, lived happily ever after, and the prime minister prospered in every way.

Other ear stories involved music and the discernment of beautiful voices and melodies. One time two gods, Apollo and Pan, argued over their musical abilities. Finally, they asked Midas to judge a contest between them. When Midas selected Pan the victor, Apollo cursed Midas with the ears of an ass since he had shown such poor judgment.

For a different kind of fable, let us turn to the Pennsylvania Dutch and their folk character Eileschpijjel. He was the source of many intriguing stories, sometimes wise, more often foolish, and always humorous. Once Eileschpijjel encountered a pumpkin which perfectly bewildered him. He never had seen such a strange thing. Fortunately a passing stranger intervened and informed Eileschpijjel that the pumpkin was a mule's egg. The stranger further advised Eileschpijjel that if he sat on the pumpkin for three weeks he would hatch a beautiful baby mule. Eileschpijjel pondered on this for a few moments and concluded that mule-hatching might be worth the while.

He sat down and squatted upon the pumpkin for several time-consuming and monotonous hours. Then he became bored with the maternal duties of incubation. He stood up and booted the pumpkin down the hillside. Tumbling end over end and sideways down the slope, the pumpkin crashed into a large tree and burst into a thousand pieces. At the same moment, a jackrabbit, hearing the dull and soggy thud of the pumpkin hitting the tree and seeing the pieces of pumpkin flying in every direction, scampered off for dear life. His ears stuck straight up, as if frozen from fear. Seeing the rabbit ear tips darting through the thicket, Eileschpijjel cried out:

"Hee-haw little colt, here is your mammy."

The Greeks had a similar story. A farmer from Kalamonti went to a greengrocer to buy a watermelon. He was astonished at the price being demanded by the shopowner. The farmer heckled the grocer and asked, "What makes this melon so dear?" The grocer responded, "This is no ordinary melon. This is a mule's mother and she is in full foal!"

The farmer, thinking he had come upon a good bargain, purchased the melon and set out for home. As he was walking home, the melon became quite heavy. As the farmer tried to change grip, the melon fell to the ground and splattered into a thousand pieces. Lo and behold, a jackrabbit, taking his cue from the flying debris, leaped out the ditch and scurried away. The farmer shouted, "Halt! You're mine!"

But the rabbit refused to heed the order. Then the farmer picked up the pieces and proceeded home. When he arrived, his wife asked, "Well, what have you there?" He murmured: "It's a mule's mother. It foaled on the way and the foal ran away." She said: "What a pity! I could have ridden it to the festivals."

More than a pumpkin or a watermelon, the eggplant does appear more like one would imagine a mule's egg to look like, if there was such a thing. And indeed, in many rural areas, eggplant is often called a mule's egg. It should also be said at this point that a jackrabbit gets its name from the jackass and the big ears they have in common.

Another story came from Haiti and the Dominican Republic. The story highlighted the frequent association of the mule with witches. The mule is often depicted as the alter ego of a witch. Once upon a time, a Dominican farmer who lived on the border between Haiti and the Dominican Republic wished to visit Haiti with his daughter and learn about voodoo. Many Dominicans were fascinated by the voodoo stories they heard emandating from Haiti. So father and daughter left Haiti on a mule. When they arrived in Haiti, the daughter disappeared. When the father turned, he saw only his mule.

After much searching, the father was told that his daughter had been captured by a witch who had converted the girl into a mother mule. The father was further informed that the mother mule was eating grass in a nearby park. He was cautioned that, if he wanted his daughter back and the witch expelled, he must promise to return to the Dominican Republic at once. If he obeyed the instructions, his daughter who had been turned into a mule would follow him. He was also told that if he should look back at any time the spell would be broken and he would never see his daughter again. He could only look back once he crossed the Artibonito bridge into the Dominican Republic. The father mounted his mule and rode to the park.

He found a mule eating flowers just as he had been told. He tied the mule to his own and started home. He was haunted by the old wives' tales which told of men who never returned home because they had doubted. With these thoughts in mind and also thoughts about his dear daughter, the father kept on his course. He wanted to turn and see if his daughter was still following.

When he came to the middle of the Artibonito bridge, the second mule stopped and made a loud, blood curdling noise. The father jumped off his mule and turned and saw his daughter. He was so excited and overcome with joy that he let go of the reins. Both mules ran away into the woods. But the father and daughter were so happy that they didn't mind walking the rest of the way home.

Another interesting mythological story came out of Spain wherein a mule became confused with a Spanish Grandee. The plot began with two young boys wondering how they were going to make their way in the world after their schooling ended. It did not take one boy long to come up with a plan to cheat a mule trader and start a career of money making.

The boy deceived the trader by making the trader believe one of his mules had been changed back into human form because his term of punishment had been completed. Actually the mule had been taken into town and sold. Furthermore, the boy made the trader feel guilty over the mistreatment and cruelty with which he had treated the mule. The capstone of the deceit was making the trader believe that the boy was actually the good Grandee of Spain.

After the "Grandee" took his leave, the trader proceeded into town. When he approached the mule barn to buy a new mule to replace the one he had lost, the mule seller couldn't believe his eyes. There, in front of him, was his old mule. He whispered in the mule's ear: "I am sorry, sir. You must have done a terrible deed to be turned back into a mule."

The mule looked up at him and the man recognized the mule's smile. He quickly decided to buy the mule once again and he promised better care to the mule since he was now aware that it actually was the Grandee of Spain. (Adapted by Amy Friedman).

In the last few decades, many articles and books have been written on what constitutes leadership and how greatness is achieved and recognized. These writings have stressed the importance of the person's ability to generate myths about their accomplishments. Great leaders caused wonderful stories about their lives. By this criterion, the mule certainly has established his claim to "greatness."

Chapter Fourteen

Mule Tails

You won't believe this, but this story is largely facts."
Bill McVean.

Many stories and jokes have been told about mules and the people associated with them. The number of stories and the humor reveal how intimately the mule affected the lives of people. Most of the jokes today that involve the mule or jackass are political in nature. Or, because of the contemporary fixation on sex, the stories have to do with sexual mores.

In the course of many years of research on the mule, Professor Burkhart gathered many of these stories. A few of them are included here for amusement and for increasing the reader's endearment with this gifted animal.

Because the rivalry between horse and mule owners was so intense, many stories revolved around the superiority of one or the other. Very often the plot had to do with racing and which animal could outrun the other. The mule people felt deep resentment over the discrimination which prevented the mule from entering many of the races and shows. Consequently, they took great delight in their victories when the barriers were let down and they were given the opportunity to prove the ability of the mule.

Clyde E. Denton told about "Old Red," the mule that never lost a race. Old Red was the perfect picture of a worn-out mule. Denton said that he "...was the most ridiculous-looking mule" that he had ever seen. "He was a tall red animal with the longest ears imaginable. His hip bones protruded at right angles to his body. His knobby knees looked like large knots on a sapling. He head hung down in an attitude of perpetual humility and he had a nervous habit of twitching first one ear and then the other, but in opposite directions."

Old Red was an easy animal to taunt because there were so many aspects about him that were grossly unusual. It was not unusual for the

141

crowd to holler at the jockey and tell him to tie a lantern on the mule's tail so they could see him come in.

Most disconcerting of all, Old Red had the habit of letting all the other entries start off the race while he just stood there for a moment to let the dust settle. Then he would start running, gradually gathering more and more momentum. By the end, he would have passed all the other racers and would win by 5 or 6 lengths. Then he would stop dead still, not wanting to exert himself more than was absolutely necessary. Satchel Paige must have taken lessons from this champion.

So aggravated and upset were the horse fanciers by these tactics, as one can imagine, that they tried all kinds of manuevers to bring about the defeat of Old Red. They would make him carry extra weight. Finally, they even made him start from fifteen feet behind the other entrants. But no matter, Old Red still won. He maintained his disturbing habit of always running just fast enough to win.

Denton concluded by condemning the injustice of Old Red's treatment. Today, hardly anyone knows of his achievements, very few people know where he is buried, and there are no monuments such as those for Man-O-War. Such has been the fate of this undefeated Champion. If he had been a horse, Denton was sure the recognition would have been quite different.

One of the most famous races between horse and mule originated in Auburn, California. J.A. Filcher recorded the encounter. One evening two teamsters were watering their animals at the same well at the Bishop Hotel near Auburn. One of the teamsters was tending a horse which "...had suffered many ailments and carried the marks and scars of hard usage. His ribs stood out like lattice on the windows of a country house; his saw-tooth back was covered with scabs and sores; he had a poke neck, cracked hoofs and stiff and swollen joints; a different limp in each leg gave him a wabbly, winding motion, which, added to the side crook in his neck, left you in doubt as to the direction he was going.

"The scars on the mule, if possible, were thicker than on the horse. One of his legs had been broken and set crooked so that the toe of his shoe had to be built on the side of the foot. He had no hair on his tail and little on his body. One eye was knocked out and there was a scum over the other. His ears lopped down by the side of his head, one falling forward and the other backward; several ribs were broken in and pressing on his lungs. They gave to his breathing a sound not unlike the combined snore of ten tired miners."

As the two men tended their steeds, they began to taunt each other about the condition of their animals. Before one could blink an eye, they were wagering a hundred dollars over which animal could outrace the other. After some negotiations, the race was to start in Auburn, go to Sacramento, round the 9th Street park, and return to Auburn. The distance was 70 miles total.

Local teamsters were well acquainted with the two animals and had argued often over which was the poorest animal on the road. Nevertheless, the race aroused great interest, speculations, calculations and argument. "The sporting community quit their poker games, their monte and their faro to take a hand in the race, and miners came up from their claims to learn more about the animals and wager their dust on the outcome."

By the time of the race, thousands of people were involved in Auburn and Sacramento and all points in between. The excitement could not have been greater had the contestants been Kentucky thoroughbreds.

"The horse was quicker in starting and at once took the lead." It got worse fast for the mule. At each mile post the mule was further behind so by the time of the ten mile post, the mule trailed by over a mile. The mule backers became slightly disheartened while the horse supporters wanted to double or triple the original bets.

"About ten o'clock at night the horse was reported five miles out of town." No one knew how far back the mule had fallen and so the victory celebration began to take shape.

But wait! "The old horse had his nose close to the ground and showed signs of great fatigue. He proceeded very slowly and at frequent intervals stopped as though anxious to give up the contest."

Then the horse stumbled and fell. His backers became a little more than nervous. "His driver laid on the whip to induce him to rise, but to no avail. Water was sent for but the beast refused to drink. His nose was sponged out and the dust washed from his eyes, and then as many strong men as could get near, after repeated efforts, succeeded in raising him to his feet.

"Slowly they were nursing him along, a few steps at a time, with a guard on either side to keep him from falling, and in this way had just reached the top of the grade when all at once a shadow and a shuffling sound came from the rear, and as the sound and the schuffle grew nearer it was discovered, to the horror of the horse men, that they were made by the mule and his driver.

143

"There had been shouts and cheers before, but nothing like those which rose from the few mule backers who were in the crowd as that old mule steadily but surely came up and, throwing a cloud of dust at every step with that ole side-wheel leg, passed the horse and took the lead in the home-stretch.

"The old brute was pretty tired...with his game leg scraping the ground and his wheezened breath almost drowning the band and the cheers, he walked across the starting line, the winner of the race....The mule was put in a comfortable stall and carefully cared for that night; and the next day, by arrangement of those who had won thousands of dollars on him, he was pensioned on a good pasture for life.

"The horse did not rise from the place where his friends had left him. Those who went out next morning to see about his welfare came back with the news that he was dead."

One more racing story involved the colorful General George Custer. It was advertised as "The Slowest and the Fastest Race in the West—or anywhere else." It was a fun event for the Army personnel at Fort Leavenworth, Kansas. The one disturbing factor was the clear contempt and low opinion of the Army officers toward the poor mule. The printed program for this affair appeared as follows:

UNITED STATES COURSE
FORT LEAVENWORTH, KANSAS
JUNE MEETING
TUESDAY, JUNE 16TH, 1868, 4 P.M.
MULE-RACE!
Officers' Purse $50
One-Mile Dash—Slow Race.

Contestants:

1. General Custer enters Hyankedank, by Hifalutin, out of Snollygester, second dam Buckjump, by Thunder, out of You Bet. Age, threescore years and ten. Colors, ring-ed, streak-ed, and strip-ed.
2. General McKeever enters Hard Tack, by Commissary, by Eaten (eatin'), second dam Contractor, by Morgan, out of Missouri. Age, forty years. Colors, purple, tipped with orange.

3. Colonel Parsons enters Symmetry (see me try), by Considerably, out of Pocket, second dam Polly Tix, by Nasby, out of Office. Age, seventeen years. Colors, uncommonly blue.
4. Captain Yates enters William Tell, by Switzerland, by Apple Tree, second dam Gessler, by Hapsburg, out of Austria. Age, eighteen years. Colors, apple green.
5. Lieutenant Leary enters Trump, by Card, out of Contractor, second dam, Leader, by Mule-Teer, out of Wagon. Age, ten years. Color, lemon.
6. Lieutenant Jackson enters Abyssinia, by Napier, out of Africa, dam Theodorus, by Solomon, out of Magdala. Age, thirty-nine years. Colors, scarlet, yellow spots.
7. Colonel Myers enters Pizzarro, by Peru, out of South America, second dam Cuzeo, by Incas, out of Andes. Age, sixteen years. Colors, light brown.
8. Lieutenant Umbstaetter enters Skirmisher, by Picket, out of Camp, second dam Carbine, by Breech Loader, out of Magazine. Age, twenty-five years. Colors, dark blue tipped in red.
9. Lieutenant Moylan enters Break-neck, by Runaway, out of Wouldn't Go, second dam Contusion, by Collision, out of Accident. Age, fifty-six. Colors, sky blue.
10. Captain Huntington enters Spavin, by Quartermaster, out of Government, second dam (not worth one). Age, twenty-one years. Colors, a-knock-to-ruin (an octoroon).
11. Lieutenant Howe enters Slow, by Tardy, out of Late, second dam, Lazy, by Inactive. Age, three times 6, four times seven, twenty eight and 11. Colors, queer.
12. Captain Weir enters Revolutionist, by Hard Luck, out of Ribmasher, second dam Blood Blister, by Can't Stand-It, our of Let's Quit. Age sixteen. Colors, black-and-blue.

Note.—The money accruing from this race is to be devoted to the support of the widows and orphans made so thereby.

Each commissioned officer could either ride in the race or pay a $5 forfeit. Major General Philip Sheridan, the post commander, did not choose to run. He decided that the mule race might tarnish his image.

After being entered, the officers proceeded to the mule pens and searched for the most lethargic, droopy-eyed mules—mules that made molasses in January look like a fastrunning creek. From past campaigns officers recalled certain slow-moving, stubborn animals that willfully held up supply trains for hours at a time. They sought out the very animals they once denounced in unprintable language.

As a major supply center from which wagon trains fanned out to other western posts, Ft. Leavenworth harbored an assortment of mules—ancient "wheelers," graying "swingers," and decrepit "leaders." Yet the mules had one thing in common. None had ever felt even the lightest touch of a saddle blanket. Hence, after each officer selected his mount, he led his would-be racer to a private area and attempted to domesticate the intractable animal.

As mentioned above, the star of this race was General George Armstrong Custer, the boy wonder of the Civil War, brevet-general at 23, major general at 25. Custer, by the way, was serving a court-martial sentence of a year's suspension of rank and pay for various irregularities and unauthorized activities.

As might be expected, the flamboyant Custer chose as his mount the crankiest mule on the post. Contrary to his alleged impetuousity on the battlefield, the general planned his mule race strategy carefully. He began by taking his ill-mannered mule to a 10 acre field and observing every move the mule made. To nullify the mule's instincts, he devised a special harness, a "mule muzzle," consisting of a leather "corset" or "wrapper" which covered the mule's chassis with innumerable leather straps.

The outraged animal was thus completely constrained. In addition to the "wrapper" there were two large "blinders" attached to the earstraps and extending over the mule's face much like an overgrown nose bag.

The good ladies of the fort turned out and so did the post band. In fact there were thousands of spectators, so many they overflowed the grandstand to the green grass surrounding the track. Shaded by giant elms, the crowd waited in tiptoe expectation.

The race was conducted by all the official rules and regulations. At the sound of the starting gun, the riders were off, but not necessarily in a forward motion. Mules shied sideways and backward. A few stood still in their shoes, refusing to move. The most irreconcilable seemed like space launching platforms, and veteran riders found themselves doing somersaults in space, landing doubled up in a heap.

For some unknown reason, the reporter of this momentous event did not record the winner of this race, that is, the one who came in last. We only were told that General Custer did not win.

Mule-Horse racing continues to the present time with much of the same intensity and rivalry. In 1976, The Great American Horse Race was held and it extended from Frankfurt, New York to Sacramento, California, a 3200 mile race. The reader guessed it. A Mule, Lord Fauntleroy, ridden by Viri Norton of San Jose, California, won the race and the $25,000 prize money. Norton was one of 94 contestants who started. He spent 315.47 hours in the saddle.

In fairness to the horse, it must be recorded that the horse sometimes won the competiion. In 1966, Abner, the horse, won The Great Omaha Horse and Mule Race. Indeed, Abner's victory marked the seventh straight time that a horse won this prestigious racing event. This race was not in Omaha, Nebraska, but in Omaha, Missouri, population, 1. Omaha is an unincorporated "wide spot in the road" in northwest Missouri that annually conducted this 10 mile race to test the sprinting superiority of horses against the superior stamina of the mules.

Robert McMorris, a columnist for the *Omaha (Nebr.) World-Herald,* reported that Abner, in winning the $500 prize, collapsed at the finish line. His handlers assured everyone that the horse would recover and be fine. One mule, named Snort, hailing from Kirksville, had pulled ahead of Abner about 50 yards from the finish line but Abner wouldn't quit. It was almost a dead heat but the horse won by a nose. Altogether there had been six mules and five horses entered, representing Iowa, Illinois, Kentucky and Missouri. Over 500 people attended and cheered the gallant participants.

Unquestionably, the race had become very popular but it still had not accomplished its original goal. Robert McCollum had organized the race to draw attention to Omaha and to force the state of Missouri to put Omaha on the map. Missouri found this difficult to accommodate because the lone resident of the "town" moved out shortly after Abner's victory.

In addition to races, there were also many contests over the strength and pulling ability of horses and mules. These contests are still an integral part of county and state fairs. Mule people love to tell stories about their mules pulling cars or tractors out of the mud or some other type of entanglement.

Thad Snow was a gifted writer, farmer and story-teller in Southeast Missouri. Mr. Snow had a mule named Kate of which he was extremely proud. He loved to talk and write about her because she was so gifted in abilities of all kinds. Snow knew that Kate was smarter than he was and he knew that Kate knew it too. But this fact did not diminish his love for Kate, it only made it greater.

One accomplishment by Kate seemed to be at the top of Snow's list. In the winter, Snow and his hired men had to load alfalfa on railroad cars. It required great effort by the men to "pinch bar" the cars an inch at a time to the proper location for loading. After performing this back-breaking work for several seasons, one of the workers wondered if the powerful Kate couldn't pull one of these boxcars by herself.

There is no adequate describing how mules look and act on a pull of that sort. They do not stand up and just pull. They get down with their bellies close to the ground. Snow and others called it "scratching" because they move their feet rapidly, only an inch at a time. There is a fast movement every instant, and it was thrilling to see.

"Kate eyed that big boxcar, and said, 'What the hell!' as plain as could be....I (Thad Snow) said, 'Kate', reassuringly, and Mose who held her line said in his squeaky voice, 'Git down and scratch.' Kate got down and scratched. She threw cinders in our faces but after a while that car moved. The rest was easy. Kate walked it a hundred yards up to our loading place with the greatest of ease. It was hell to start but easy to pull. After that we had no more use for 'pinch bars'."

Later, Kate had trouble moving one of the cars. Snow sent a work-man to make sure the brake was loosened and that there were no obstructions by the wheels. She scratched and scratched till Snow thought her great heart would burst. He had never seen anything like it. At last the car moved, then more movement, and Kate straightened up and walked on.

Everyone was watching Kate and no one noticed until she was well on her way that she had two cars and not one. The second car had not come uncoupled. Snow doubted if any other mule ever performed such a labor.

Snow said that "Kate was admired and bragged about by every man who worked her or ever saw her work. It didn't turn her head. She mellowed a little, (Snow thought), as the years went by; but she remained aloof to the end. Her work was her interest in life, and she gave it all she had."

Teamsters were greatly given to boasting. Hardly ever did they confess to the true weight of their load. They always tried to pick a figure that they thought no one else could match. It always involved the biggest loads over the roughest roads and with the least number of mules of anybody in the world.

After listening to round after round of such encounters, the men finally turned to Pete Miller who had been very quiet. Pete had a hair lip which interfered materially with his articulation, as J.A. Filcher reported. "He had the knack of making himself understood and feared by his mules, however, and was rated a first-class teamster. By reason of his infirmity of speech, of which he was rather sensitive, he seldom spoke except when he was spoken to. How much do you haul Pete?

"Me?" "Yes, Pete," said a half dozen in chorus, "how much do you haul?"

"We' I te' you bo's, I 'ink I 'arry abou' a' mu' on my wa'on a' any o' you, bu' I don' 'ink I 'arry wite so mu' i' ma mou'."

A common log hauling story was told with many different variations depending upon the circumstances. Beck, in his book, The Lore of the Lumber Camps, wrote about a lumber camp in Michigan. An Ozark woodsman had come to the camp. After the work was done one day, the boys were sitting around swapping stories about their mules and their hauling and pulling. Finally it came the turn of the lumberjack from Missouri.

He began, "That reminds me of my big mule. I was riding my mule through a swamp when I came on a team stuck while pulling a load of logs. While I sat there another team came up and hitched on. The four team hitch of horses couldn't budge it. So I asked to hook my mule to the load. Says I,

'My mule works best by himself.' So the four horses were unhitched and I hitched my mule on the load. And what do you think?"

"I think the mule pulled the load right out of the swamp," echoed the jacks.

"Nope," answered the Ozark axman, "He never budged it."

Another story involved an Ozark farmer who was so poor that he had only an ox and a mule to help him. He often had to hitch the two together to get the heavy work done. One day he had them working together but the ox was laying back and not pulling his share of the load. The ox thought he was being very clever. At the end of the day, when the farmer put them in their stalls, the ox thought for sure the mule would complain about having to do all the work that day. But the mule said nothing. The next day, the ox repeated his performance since it had gone so well the day before. Again the mule did not complain. So it went the third day.

That night, the ox was curious about the person that the farmer had stopped to talk to on the way home from the field. So he asked the mule who the man was. The mule simply replied that it was an old friend of the farmer, the butcher. From then on, the ox pulled his share of the load.

Country and small town boys are always looking for pranks to pull on people of authority. Back in the middle of the Prohibition Days, Dick Blank of Regan, Nebraska purchased a big white mule at an auction over behind Stamford. Before he got the mule home, Dick realized the creature was an outlaw killer who should be returned at once to the open plains. The animal would whirl and prance, stand on his front feet and kick like all fury.

Almost as soon as Dick stabled the animal in his barn, his friends knew about the white mule with the black disposition. With the insidious traits of the mule in mind, Dick's friends artfully reported to the Constable the undeniable fact that Dick Blank had hidden some "white mule" in his barn. They spiced up the situation by adding that Dick was planning a big party.

The Marshall was eager to make an arrest and took the story just as the pranksters hoped he would. Waiting until nightfall, the law officer, armed with a flashlight, slipped quietly down a back alley. When he came to Dick Blank's barn, he opened the door, stepped inside, and flashed the light. He immediately received indisputable evidence that this "white mule" had quite a kick in it.

The Constable recovered himself as best he could and managed to crawl out of the barn. He went home by a devious route to avoid the fellows who were waiting at the corner of the livery stable to give him not the usual horse laugh but an air splitting mule bray.

Some people have seen a white mule and others have drunk it, and a few have drunk enough to see pink elephants, but fewer still have drunk so much as to see pink mules. Nevertheless, in the town of Orleans, Nebraska, not far from Regan, a number of influential and respectable people, sufficient by far to remove the matter from the realm of the apparition, witnessed this phenomenon and witnessed it in broad daylight.

Fifty years ago, after one of Nebraska's famous winter storms, when it snowed so hard the drifts covered the horns of the cattle, the son of a local farmer hitched a pair of his father's mules to a bobsled, filled the sled with fresh hay, and covered the hay with two large red comforts, fringed with knitting yarn. That night he invited a score or more of young people to go on a sleigh ride. The mules were white and as they sped over the snow in the darkness they were practically invisible.

As might be anticipated, the young people drove too fast and when the sled reached Stamford, seven miles away, the mules were covered with a lather of sweat. The sleighing party pulled up in front of the only restaurant which was open at that time. The group jumped off the sleigh and went inside for refreshments. The son, the driver, ever mindful of the proper care of farm animals, blanketed the mules with the two red-outing, flannel quilts, and then joined the rest of the party.

It was over an hour later when the sleighers emerged from the cafe, warm and ready for the return trip. When the red comforts were removed from the backs of the mules, no one noticed in the darkness that the red quilts had faded into the white hair of the damp mules. The mules were dyed a pink pastel, matching the shade of early cherry blossoms. All of the asthetic effects, however, were lost on the sleighers. The change remained undetected even when the mules were unharnessed in the utter darkness of the stock barn back at the farm.

The next morning, the son slept late and the chore of hitching the mules for a quick trip to town fell to the hired man. It so happened that this hired man was color-blind. He was unaware of the fairy-like color and character of his team. The driver paced them sprightly down the road and into town. The early morning shoppers stopped, looked, shook their heads, and looked again. They stared. Unmindful of the scene he was creating, the driver pulled his team to a halt in front of the local saloon.

The first person to emerge from the local watering hole, after having had his fresherupper, was the town alcoholic. He took one look at the pink mules, walked back into the bar, picked up the bottle from which he had been drinking, and smashed it over the hard oak bar. Then he walked out of the establishment straighter than he had ever walked before and headed for the Methodist Church. Here he joined the Lincoln-Lee Legion and took the pledge. Not trusting his moral powers and ethical convictions, the man took the first train out of town for Dwight, Illinois, where he underwent the Keely Cure.

Another time in another place, a weary traveler was walking down a hot dusty road at noonday in the middle of a crop-searing July heat wave. Almost as if in answer to his prayers, the wayfarer saw a well pump not far away in a roadside pasture. Hurdling the fence, the stranger made his way to the well. While he was pumping he noticed a mule standing about thirty feet away. As the traveler lifted the tin cup of water to his lips, he heard: "Sir, would you mind pumping me about a gallon of that stuff?" The cup fell out of his hand. He could not believe his ears, but as he turned around toward the mule, the animal spoke again: "I'm hot too you know."

The stranger hastily pumped a bucket of water for the mule and then beat a quick retreat to the road. At the nearby farmhouse, he saw a farmer feeding his hogs. After exchanging greetings, the passerby commented about the weather: "It's mighty dry and hot around these parts."

"Yes," replied the farmer, "It's so dry I hear the hard-shell Baptists have resorted to sprinkling, and the Presbyterians are using a damp cloth." The traveller paused a moment, and then came directly to the point. "That's a remarkable animal you have out there in the pasture."

"Oh", said the farmer, "You mean that mule. He's alright. He's as gentle as a lamb. The only thing is you can't believe everything he says. Don't you believe that yarn he tells about building the Panama Canal."

Another talking mule story with more of a colloquial touch is quoted in Botkin's book of American Folklore. Appropriately, perhaps, the story is included under the heading: "Wit and Nitwit".

Every morning a farmer or his son would go to the pasture to fetch the mule named Bill. They would call out: "Come round, Bill". One morning, Bill got tired of this greeting and he complained to the son about being called in this manner. Of course, the boy was startled to hear the mule talk. He ran back to the house and reported to his father what had happened. The father thought his son was being lazy and didn't want to fetch the mule. But he did go to the pasture to see for himself.

After the usual greeting, Bill voiced his complaint once again. The father and his little dog were startled. They began running. When they reached exhaustion, the old man and his dog sat down on the ground to rest. The dog looked up and said: "I didn't know a mule could talk." At that the father started running again and is still running as far as anyone knows.

Before one starts mumbling about the absurdity of "talking mules or asses," please consider this account straight from the Bible. In one of the few cases of a speaking animal in the Bible, Balaam, the Prophet, engaged in a dialogue with his faithful donkey. Walking along a well traveled path, the donkey suddenly stopped at the sight of the angel of the Lord, who stood in dazzling splendor in the middle of the path.

Thinking the donkey was simply recalcitrant and stubborn, Balaam began to beat and berate the animal. The donkey caustically asked:

"Am I not thine ass upon which thou hast ridden all thy life long unto this day? Was I ever want to do so unto thee?"

Balaam reluctantly admitted that he had never known his donkey to be stubborn before. At that time, Balaam's eyes were opened and he saw and heard the angel. The angel informed Balaam that if the donkey had not stopped, "I surely just now would have slain you."

So the moral of the account is quite clear. When an ass or a mule speaks, one had better pay attention and heed carefully the message.

If some people sometimes drink too much, it happened one time that a mule drank too much. Cecil Smith had a farm in Smithton, Missouri, and one year the potato bugs were destroying a very fine crop of potatoes. Cecil consulted the *Farmers' Almanac* to learn how to handle the situation.

Following the clear instructions, Cecil mixed up twelve gallons of arsenic of lead, filled a two gallon spray can, and proceeded to spray the potato vines. Just as he was finishing, he heard a loud sucking noise which indicated the bottom of the barrel had been reached. The farmer turned and saw his mule finishing off the last few drops. He had drunk ten gallons of the poisonous mixture.

As quick as he could, Cecil called Dr. Reynolds and explained what had happened, that the mule had drunk 10 gallons of arsenic of lead. "Ten gallons?" asked the doctor, "That's good." The doctor went on to explain, "he's drunk too much to hurt him. If he had just drunk a little of the liquid it would have killed him, but now I am sure he is going to be alright."

Sure enough, in a couple of days, the mule was back to normal, with one exception. Previously the mule had been infected with bots and other intestinal parasites. The arsenic of lead relieved the mule of all of his internal disabilities, and he soon became the healthiest mule on the farm.

Speaking of medicine, a clever veterinarian thought he had devised a sure and pat method for getting mules to take pills. He merely inserted a long tube into the throat of the animal he was treating, and then himself blew the pill down. He achieved great fame and recognition for his easy solution for a big problem.

Then, one day, he met up with a recalcitrant mule as a patient. The mule needed a pill. The tube was injected, but just as the doctor was ready to blow, the mule belched! The saddened vet learned the hard way that there is no easy solution to a mule problem.

Down in southern Missouri, there once was a mule with a very disconcerting spot. The mule belonged to "Zeke" Eliason. Zeke was a normal young man who had gone through all the trials and tribulations of a young person growing up and trying to find himself. Some people had called him incorrigible and beyond hope. But then he met Sally Black, a beautiful girl who was as good as Zeke had been bad.

Sally did what the preacher couldn't do, she reformed Zeke into a sincere church going citizen. He began to squire Sally to church on Sunday and, for good measure, to Wednesday night prayer meeting too.

Except for Sally, Zeke's only other object of affection was his mule. The animal was big, black as the ace of spades, bright-eyed, white-nosed, and had the fanciest style of any mule anywhere. The mule's only blemish was a small spot of white hair right beneath his tail. However, the spot didn't show at all except when the mule raised his tail, and when he did, the white spot looked positively indecent. Fortunately, most of the time, the mule had enough sense to keep his tail modestly low.

Every Sunday, Zeke would hitch up his mule to pick up Sally and go to church. Invariably Sally was waiting in her white dress, just as full of anticipation as Zeke was. It did not take but the slightest touch of the whip for the mule to know he was headed for church. Along the way was a wild cherry tree on which the mule liked to nibble a few leaves and where he relieved himself. Every time he did so, the white spot showed like sin. It embarrassed Zeke and he was afraid Sally was mortified at the very sight.

Zeke was never sure that Sally actually saw the spot. If she did, she never mentioned the obscenity. Nonetheless, Zeke saw it and he was frightfully put out. Every time the embarrassment seemed to get greater.

Finally Zeke got up earlier than usual one Sunday morning and decided to do something about the white spot. After harnessing his mule, Zeke applied some black shoe polish to the white hair and colored it black. It looked like a pretty good job. He had butterflies about the whole affair but he hoped it would cure the problem.

Zeke picked up Sally as usual and they headed for church. They came to the wild cheery tree and the mule did his duty. Lo and behold, the spot didn't show. Everything was perfect. They attended church and the trip home was uneventful. When they arrived at Sally's home, Zeke jumped out in one bound and helped Sally down from the buggy seat. They walked to the house and Sally didn't utter a word until she reached the front door and turned to say goodbye.

"Zeke, you wouldn't have swapped that mule, would you?"

Zeke's eyes just about popped out and he couldn't swallow. He was shocked, flustered, and bewildered. All the way home he kept wondering, "Did Sally say 'swapped' or 'swabbed'?"

In recent years, coon hunting on mules has become more and more popular in Missouri, Kansas and elsewhere. These coon hunters have a long litany of praises to sing for the way the mule performs on their outings. The language is something special to hear and enjoy.

Dave Baugh of Carthage, Missouri, provided some vivid images of coon hunting with mules. "The first time we went and treed a coon with our mules, we tied the mules probably 30 feet from the tree and squalled the coon down instead of shootin' it out. We squalled it out. Squallin' means we made a noise somethin' like a coon fightin' or somethin' like that and the old coon'll get excited, especially the bigger coon, will get excited and climb right down that tree and crawl out on the dog's head. And the fight is on....They ended up fightin' and right around our mules and everything. Didn't bother them a bit. Squallin' and abawlin' and everything else and dogs carryin' on but it didn't bother them mules a bit."

Sometimes coon hunting involved going through some rugged terrain, underbrush, and creek bed and banks. One time, Baugh's companion had a steep creek bank to climb. "I seen him get ahold of her goin' up a steep bank that he didn't wanta ride her up, he'd just turn her loose and grab ahold of her tail and walk right on up behind her. And there's quite a few of 'em, but them kind is hard to find and them kind usually don't have no price on 'em.

Were the mules ever bothered by the coon dogs? What about the mules kicking these dogs? "Yeah. And that usually 'bout the best way to break a dog to lead. They learn right quick. And we've never had one killed. The mule, I think, seems to know. They don't really try to put the hurt on 'em, but they'll let 'em know where to stay."

What about the mule kicking the hunter? "This one night this cousin of mine had took his young brother-in-law, his new brother-in-law, and he hadn't been around these mules very much and the little mule my cousin had was a very bad kickin' mule. I mean extra bad kickin' mule. She's reach out to get you, now. And none of us really liked to hunt with her 'cause you'd forget and you tie 'em up and you get excited and go to the tree and you shoot the coon out and you're lookin' up around in the air and lose your direction or somethin', you know, tryin' to find the coon and you happen to walk back out under that mule, she'll let you know right quick where she's at."

Rick Plymell from Bethany, Missouri, couldn't get over how stout the mules were and how they could haul around some pretty heavy people. "Now the boy that's bringin' these mules over here tonight, his dad, he probably stands about 5'8" and he'll weigh well over 200 pounds....He's kinda got bad feet and bad ankles, you know, and he really loves to go coon huntin' but he just couldn't hardly get around and he finally bought some mules and he said he wouldn't go coon huntin' now without a mule.

"These ole mules're stout....Heck, I 'spect his dad weighs half as much as those mules do. I doubt if they'll weigh 600 pounds or five, somethin' like that....But they can ride 'em all night long and they'll still jump fences and jump across ditches. Seemed like when the weather got cooler all the time, they was wantin' to be a little bit more frisky. They're ready to go.

"But they say that you never wanta show fear of 'em. You wanta have their whole undevoted attention whenever you're ridin' 'em because if you let 'em get by with somethin', they'll always remember it. You wanta make 'em do exactly what you want 'em to do. And when I'm goin' through the brush, I rein him up real tight and I'll take my hand and put them reins right down there on his neck, just rein tight down there on his neck and, boy, it's just like steerin' a car through the brush, or a motorcycle. It's amazin' how good they handle in the brush. You can just....I just can't hardly believe how good they handle."

Plymell warned about the kickin' though, especially when you take off the saddle. "Sometimes they'll still be full of energy and they'll be glad to get that saddle off and they'll kick....You always wanta turn 'em facin' you. 'Cause they have to spin around and then kick...they're not doin' it just because they are mean. They're just doin' it because they're glad to get the saddle off and they're stretchin' their hide out, I reckon, or just stretchin'."

One time some friends of Plymell came up from the Ozarks to coon hunt around Bethany. "It was real funny. Them mules had never been out of south Missouri. 'Course all the cricks and ditches down there are rock bottoms. A mule probably don't even sink above the knees. The first night they was ridin', they got down there on a little ole drainage ditch that goes in the crick. It was muddy anyway, and they baled off in that ditch and them mules sunk about to their bellies and I reckon one mule throwed this one ole boy and ran back to the barn.

"I mean, they were just plumb scared to death 'cause they didn't know what that mud was 'cause they was sinkin'. It took us quite a little bit to get those mules to ridin' up in here. Now we come across a little ole ditch, 3 or 4 foot acrost that's got water in the bottom of it, instead of 'em walkin' on acrost it, boy, they'll just set back and they'll jump right acrost it. Yeah, you better be hangin' on. I was ahangin' onto the saddle horn when they jump, and boy, I'm tellin' you, that one mule, he 'bout yanked me completely off, he jumped so hard."

Chapter Fifteen

Short Mule Tails

Because the mule has been such a successful and popular product, the zebra growers have tried to invade the market. Several zebra owners have bred their animals to jacks. In Madison, Wisconsin, the offspring of such a union had the striped legs of the mother, but everything else was from the jack. The new business then had the problem of what to name this "new species". Should it be Zebrule, Zony, Zonkey, or Zebrass? Or what?

———

At one point the Athenian Assembly had grown tired of Demosthenes's continual argumentation. They refused to let him continue speaking. In his defense, Demosthenes stated that he wished only to say a few words. Under this condition, the Assembly agreed. Demosthenes began: "a young man in the summertime hired a donkey to go from the city to Megara. When noon came the sun was blazing fiercely, both the young man and the owner of the donkey wished to lie down in its shadow. Each tried to prevent the other from doing so. The owner maintained that he had rented the donkey, not its shadow; and the one who hired the donkey argued that he had complete rights to him."

After saying this, Demosthenes stopped and turned away. The Athenians rushed to him and asked what was the rest of the story. Demosthenes replied: "You are willing to listen when I speak about the shadow of a jackass, but when I speak of serious matters, you refuse."

———

Frank Glenn of Columbia, Missouri once told a true story about one of his mules who had been struck by lightning. Glenn told it this way: "Lightnin' hit that mule, knocked her down in the pasture. And we was goin' to the football game and we saw it layin' over there and we turned around and went back. We got an old barn door, hooked the mules to it, and took that mule, laid it over on that barn door. It didn't kill it, but just knocked it...couldn't walk or nothin'.

So we kept that mule in the barn and we had a rubber mallet and every day or two we'd go over and hit on the back, just up and down the backbone, you know. And that mule finally got well and made one of the best work mules I ever saw in my life. And ita'd be hot, a hundred degrees, and that mule'd never take a long breath. Funniest thing. The other mules'd be pantin' and it wouldn't....It wobbled when it walked. Wobbled. We called it "Lightning"!

———————

Some farmers up around Bethany, Missouri were considering the purchase of a new binder. These farmers had been performing the operation of tying wheat bundles by hand. They had heard that Sam Fogleman over in Mercer County had bought one of the new binders, so they were over to his farm to see how it worked. At the time of their arrival, Fogleman had the new binder in operation in his wheat field. When the visitors appeared, the mules pulling the binder became frightened and ran away, cutting through the middle of the wheat field. "The wire binder never missed a bundle in the wild dash of the mules. That was enough to convince the visitors that the new device was practical, and also soundly constructed." They returned home and ordered one for their farm.

———————

"City finances have been given a slight shot in the arm by a team of mules that refuses to die." So began a news article in the *St. Louis Post Dispatch*. "The situation came to light when the Budget Director, E. G. Schubkegel, approved the request of Walter Fath...to transfer $400 from Account 17B to Account 14A. Account 17B, which has been included in the Meramec Hills budget for the last several years, is for the purchase of two mules to replace the old pair now in use at the school. Account 14A is for maintenance and repairs. Fath hoped that the ancient team would live another year.

The school district inherited the mules more than 20 years ago when the city abandoned use of mules to draw garbage wagons. They are so old they had numbers rather than names, and the numbers long since have been forgotten."

In France, there is fairly common superstition that it is good luck to kiss the cards before playing a game. In Denmark, there is a superstition that if you drop a piece of bread on the floor you must quickly pick it up and kiss it for luck. And in Germany, it was once thought that a toothache could be cured by kissing a jackass.

Concerning the difference between a man and the jackass, some observers hold that there isn't any. But this opinion wrongs the jackass. (Mark Twain).

Suppose you were president of the United States. Suppose you were an idiot. But then I repeat myself. (Mark Twain).

Sometimes bad things happen but have good results. A man in Missouri wanted desperately to be elected to Congress. But he used such big words in his campaign speeches that his fellow citizens couldn't understand him. The polls indicated that he would have little chance to win the election. Then it happened that a mule kicked him in the jaw, causing him to bite off the tip of his tongue. After that he could use only one syllable words and he made such a hit with the farmers, he got elected. (Mark Twain).

Some Ozarkians explain the meaning of primary elections this way. They are called "Primaries" because that's the grade level of the politicians.

A farmer, concerned about well meaning tourists who fed his mule, pinned a notice to his fence: "Please do not feed treats to the mule." Signed: The Owner.

Shortly afterward, another notice appeared below the first. It read: "Please pay no attention to the above notice."

Signed, the Mule.

The Illinois farm newspaper, *Farm Impact*, had this equation for young math enthusiasts:

$$\begin{array}{r} 1 \ \text{Jack} \\ + \ 1 \ \text{Mare} \\ \hline 1 \ \text{Mule} \end{array}$$

At one time all the street cars in Chicago and St. Louis were pulled by mules, and some horses, but mainly mules. They were referred to as hay burners. Then electricity came along and the trolley car and a lot of mules were unemployed. A Joplin, Missouri citizen travelled to East St. Louis just as the street car company had retired some mules and replaced them with electric cars. He went in the mule barn and there were the mules switching their tails, eating, and an old-time negro was in the mule barn and seeing Mr. Jacobs said: "Look at those mules. Aren't those Yankees wonderful. First they came down here and freed us colored folk and now they bring electricity and emancipate the hard workin' mule. Electricity is great. If we didn't have any you know we would still be watchin' color television by candlelight."

One old timer had a mule that limped sometimes and walked alright other times. So the old timer asked the vet what to do about this condition. The vet prescribed that the old timer watch the mule carefully and when she walks alright, catch her and sell her.

On the television show, Gunsmoke, Festus had a mule by the name of Ruth. Once Festus was leaving town and saying good-bye to Newly who said: "Now take it slow and easy, Festus." To which Festus replied: "Wael now, them's the onlyest two gaits Ruth's got—slow and easy."

Whenever Festus received a letter, he would invariably say that he would have to wait until Ruth read the letter to him so he could understand what the letter said.

———

A Missouri farmer, when told that the Missouri Mule was vanishing and that the end of the mule was near, was supposed to have said: "Yes, it is true that the mule is disappearing. However, it does seem that horses' asses and jackasses are increasing by the minute."

———

During the flood of 1993, G.I. Smith had his picture in the *St. Louis Post-Dispatch* along with his mule. Smith was abandoning his house and yard. His escape was by boat which was being pulled by a mule who was up to his belly in water. One never knows what a mule will be asked to do.

———

Carl Russell of Galt, Missouri, used to say that his two mules, Maude and Warrior, were "just as ornery as he was."

Russell also gave this advice: "The first thing with a mule when you get him in to break him is to learn him his name. You know you can't do that in the barn with the rest of them. Take him out behind the barn with a good strap and teach him his name, first thing. They have to know their name when you speak to them."

———

Homer Croy said that a mule gets notions sometimes. He wouldn't be a mule if he didn't.

It takes a long time to learn mules. "You never learn them—" I've watched them a lifetime, but I'm still in the first reader."

Croy added: "In talking about mules, mule men always hedged. They'd say that a fella can go wrong mighty easy on mules. My feeling is this way but...on the other hand, I heard statements by good mule men that tended just the opposite."

———

David Rankin may have had the biggest farm in Missouri history. He owned and farmed about 36,000 acres in the northwest corner of the state, by Tarkio. He used 1,000 mules. One corn field was 6,000 acres. Special trains brought sight seers from the St. Louis Fair to see this unusual corn field. Rankin probably invented the "two-row cultivator." Not only was he creative in his farming techniques, but he was a meticulous administrator. He seemed to know everything that was going on everywhere on his farm.

———

Writer Samuel Bowles had an interesting proof for the idea of "transmigration of souls." Bowles was convinced that he knew quite a few people who must have been mules at one time.

Bowles also admitted that he had had many arguments with mules. He ended up not winning one of them.

———

During World War I, a clever cartoon appeared in the *New Yorker*. There were four panels in the cartoon and in each panel the were four mules standing side by side. In the bottom panel, one of the mules had kicked a corporal and the four mules were laughing. In the second panel, one of the mules had kicked a sergeant and the four mules laughed with more vigor. In the third panel, one of the mules kicked a captain, and the mules laughed even more vigorously. In the fourth panel, one of the mules kicked a Colonel, and then the mules really rolled with laughter.

———

During the stock market crash, a Missourian had been asked if he had been a bear or a bull in the market. He replied:
"Neither. I was a JACKASS."

The *Saturday Evening Post* asked the reader to judge the following case: "Tom, who owned the laziest mule in the county, one day borrowed his neighbor Fred's hard-working mule to do some plowing which required a two-mule hitch. It was an unseasonably hot day. Between the heat and having to do too much pulling, the borrowed animal fell dead. Fred later sued Tom for his mule's value, $500.

'Having borrowed my good mule, he was duty-bound to take care of her,' Fred contended. 'Instead, he let her work herself to death in the heat while his lazy beast loafed along.'

'Everybody knows that no two mules work alike and that one always will pull harder than the other,' Tom replied nonchalantly. 'I didn't drive his mule harder than my own. It was her own nature that made her work so. Therefore I am not responsible for her death.'

The jury decided that Tom had to pay. After much deliberation, the jury decided that it is negligent to permit a mule to work itself to death while its teammate loafs."

An old Irish Blessing:

May you have:
No Frost on your Spuds.
No Worms on your Cabbage.
May your Goat give Plenty of Milk.
If you inherit a Donkey, may she be in foal.

A muleskinner called himself a "senior" but he didn't look forward to "graduation."

Retired Professor of Languages Al Delmez remembers a short verse that he learned as a young boy in southeast Kansas. He can't explain why he committed it to memory but it has stayed with him all these years:

A mule in a barn, lazy and sick,
Boy with a nail on the end of a stick,
Boy jabs mule, mule makes lurch,
Services monday at the M. E. Church.

Some critics complain about many current biographers being guilty of "reductionism." After studying a person's life thoroughly, the author picks out one idea or thing that explains everything about the subject. The whole biography hinges on this idea or theme.

One doesn't have to worry about reductionism being employed to explain mules. Everyone knows this complicated animal cannot be explained by a single theme or idea.

Once a mule trader telling a story was challenged by an eyewitness about the truthfulness of his account. The mule trader exclaimed: "Goddam an eyewitness anyway—He always spoils a good story."

Harry Truman once gave a good mulish description of a press conference. "Some damn-fool reporter would ask me a damn-fool question and I'd give some damn-fool answer."

After President Clinton made a rousing speech to the nation, the press called it a real "marching speech" and the president was calling cadence loud and clear, left-right-left-right. The troops clearly were to fall in line and support him. Of course, the mule would have corrected the president with gee-haw, gee-haw.

Recent newspaper articles which underscored President Clinton's vote-buying practices with Congressional members emphasized the fact that political mule-trading was as old as, well, mules.

––––––––––

Donkeys and elephants still create a political occasion. In early April of 1995, the Ringling Bros. and Barnum and Bailey Circus came to Washington D.C. Photographers and journalists couldn't resist the temptation so they lined up at least ten elephants in front of the nation's capitol building. Each elephant stood on its hind legs with its front legs on the elephant in front of it. The picture made the front page of many newspapers across the country including the *St. Louis Post-Dispatch,* April 6, 1995.

––––––––––

In Fairplay, Colorado, Republican Ken Chlouber engaged in a burro race awith his Democratic opponent, Curtis Imrie. The race was staged so as to draw more attention to the upcoming election. Imrie tried to get his GOP rival to ride a pachyderm but everyone agreed how unfair this would be to the Republicans.

The fact that these contests still happen in the 1990s is ample testimony to the staying power of the party symbols.

––––––––––

In the world of mules, there are no rules. Ogden Nash

––––––––––

The Mule is good work and bad trouble. Pennsylvania Dutch proverb.

––––––––––

The Mule that pulls the plow gets the fodder and the straw; the saddle horse gets the fancy oats. Missouri Folk saying.

––––––––––

Guy Simmons wrote a poem wherein he recounted all the ways his mule had bedeviled him over the years. Having bought a new tractor, Guy could now get rid of the mule. He recalled how the mule had destroyed his new plow by wrappin' it around a 'simmon tree and how the renegade had kicked him in the jaw. But now Guy could get even. Actually, Guy was turning the mule out to pasture so he could enjoy its remaining years. Guy taunted the mule at the end by saying that the mule would never be as happy as when it was causing Guy trouble.

Chapter Sixteen

The Mule and Harry S. Truman

This millennium coincides with a special time for the world and for America. With the end of the Cold War and the collapse of the Soviet Union, America is searching for new policies and new directions to cope with the many political, economic, social and cultural problems that confront the world. New technologies and an almost instantaneous world-wide communication system have introduced so much rapid change that it is almost impossible to cope rationally and coherently with so much newness. In the midst of this malaise, it is certainly interesting to see so many Americans develop a special attraction to Harry S Truman. These people are saying that we need a new Truman to lead us now. And even more amazing, this attraction is non-partisan as both political parties pay him homage.

Photograph by Marvin Kreisman

"Yes, Mr. President, the mule kicks as hard as ever."

Why is this so? Since Watergate and the intervening double-talk disasters, the public wants some truthful and straight talk from their president and other political leaders. Truman is known as "Give 'em Hell Harry." He always explained this phenomenon by saying that he spoke the truth and his enemies thought that was "hell." Truman pulled no punches; he lacked Roosevelt's gracious manner and art of dissembling. Like the mule, Truman's style had a powerful kick. He once wrote to Dean Acheson that "he liked to kick ass," to get things moving.

Truman was from Missouri and so much of his character, speech, and manner were shaped by that very fact. Truman has been praised as the Common Man, the Everyday American, the Ordinary Citizen, or the Middle American. Walter Lippmann called him a "provincial American." Missourians are often described this way because Missouri is in the center of America. Many images project it as the "Heart of America." Although this is true, many parts of the country do not want to claim its centerpoint. Easterners say it is "out west;" westerners say it is "back east;" northerners say it is "down south;" and southerners say it "up north."

Throughout much of the 19th century, Missouri was the "gateway," the funnel, through which easterners and southerners poured westward. The three great trails west took off from Missouri: The Santa Fe Trail, The Oregon Trail, and the Overland Trail. Some authors have called Missouri the Mother of the West. The mule played an important role in this great migration and by the end of century, all American mules were called Missouri Mules no matter where their origin may have been.

Like the Missouri Mule, Truman was known for his endurance and toughness. Many observers said that he had a tough hide. He worked long hours to keep up with his many responsibilities. Many people questioned his intellectual capacity to function as president, but Truman said he had the job and he would give it his best effort. One aide said that Truman approached each day with spirit and dedication. Somehow he believed that it would work out. In Missouri, there is a plentiful supply of "Osage Orange," or hedge wood. This wood is one of the toughest and most durable of woods. In a wood stove, it can generate so much heat that it can ruin the stove. Indians used it to make their bows. Some farmers said that the mule was made of Osage Orange; some Missouri politicians knew that Truman was made of it too.

When Truman was born, his father put a mule shoe over the front door for good luck. This is probably an apocryphal story but it easily could have been true. His father was a mule trader. Harry learned from him how to tell the age of a mule or horse by looking at their teeth. Once in the 1948 presidential campaign, Truman stopped a parade in Oklahoma to look at the mouth of a beautiful Palomino who was stealing the audience's attention. Truman announced the horse's age to be six, and the rider affirmed it with great enthusiasm and approval for Truman's ability.

Also in 1948, Truman won innumerable farm votes by showing his genuine farming background. At a big farm gathering in Dexter, Iowa, one of the host farmers was wondering how big the crowd was. Without a moment's hesitation, Truman reasoned out loud that the field was 80 acres and an acre would hold about 1,000 people, so there were approximately 80,000 people in attendance. If that Iowa farmer ever doubted Truman's farm credentials, those doubts were dispelled then and there. Over and over, his small town, human touch won him support. He was genuine American.

Like the mule, Truman could also be stubborn, and in much the same way. Muleskinners said the mule was stubborn and refused to do something because he often knew something the muleskinner didn't know. The mule was aware of the presence of a rattlesnake long before the muleskinner. And the same was true for many other dangers. The mule had great determination. It was hard to change his mind once it was set. Churchill said that Truman had great determination, especially at Potsdam. Churchill said that he was much like the famous Missouri Mule.

Both Truman and the mule were perennial underdogs. The mule always suffered by comparison to the horse who was much more handsome and attractive to the eye. The horse had style and class. In the literature of the American West there are countless stories about races between the horse and the mule. Strangely enough, the mule often won because of its endurance and the overconfidence of the people handling the horse. Does that sound like the 1948 race for the presidency?

One more common note between the mule and Truman has to do with language. Because of their independent and stubborn behavior, the mule provoked many farmers and muleskinners to a high level of swearing proficiency. Truman probably reached the 33rd degree in this skill. As a farmer and artillery officer, it served him well. As president, it had mixed results. Many condemned him because of his vulgarity which they thought unbecoming a president. On the other hand, it endeared him to many Americans because it was such a normal way to release emotion in a tight, hard-hitting fight. One muleskinner admitted that he could talk to his mules like St. John Chrysostom, the saint with the "golden tongue" in talking about the mysteries of God, but it wouldn't be very effective. Missouri politicians reasoned the same way when they were in a political campaign. In his first senatorial campaign in 1934, it was said that Truman hurled devastating fire at his opponents. "Give 'em Hell Harry" was at work long before 1948.

Once Truman was showing Bess' bridge group around the Rose Garden at the White House. Truman pointed out the different kinds of manure used in the garden. Later one of the women complained to Bess about the president using the word manure. Bess replied: "You don't know how long it took me to make him use the word manure."

The story illustrated the earthiness and commonness of Truman which many Americans now view in a positive way. The man from Missouri gave clear witness to the power of the simple virtues: hard work, honesty, determination, candor, perseverance, durability, and humor. Truman has become the epitome of a simple way of life. When he left the White House, he came home to Independence and associated freely and happily with his former friends. Visitors to the Truman home on Delaware Street are amazed at the simple, everyday furniture and surroundings. Mary McGrory, a Washington columnist, wrote about Truman: "He did not require to be loved. He did not expect to be followed blindly. Congressional opposition never struck him as subversive, nor did he regard his critics as traitors. He never whined." Admiral King, who had served both Roosevelt and Truman, said that Truman was a more typical American than Roosevelt, and the Admiral implied that it gave Truman an advantage as he became president. From the mule, he had learned that a person had to have the ability to stay with a job until it was done. One had to have an inner iron, a bedrock of determination and stubborn will power.

Americans have found humor to be a most effective way to deal with difficult situations. This tendency is especially evident among the country's political leaders. The mule and jackass have provided endless opportunities for making a point or turning aside a criticism. The fact that these animals still appear so frequently in cartoons, stories and jokes indicates some special qualities that seem to be integral to American life and style.

If America can rededicate itself to the old mulish and "Middle-American" virtues of hard work, simplicity, stubborn perseverance and adaptability, hope can be strong for the next millennium.